THE

Chanson de Roland

THE

Chanson de Roland

PIERRE LE GENTIL

Translated from the French by
Frances F. Beer

HARVARD UNIVERSITY PRESS
Cambridge, Massachusetts
1969

FOREWORD

Among the masterpieces of medieval literature, the *Chanson de Roland* is more than a simple title cited with indifference. Even the most unsophisticated Frenchman remembers the wonderful scene of the hero's death with emotion; those who are not satisfied with remembering, but reread the poem to understand it more fully, are becoming increasingly numerous. And scholars continue passionately to discuss it. Still, although the curiosity of the general public has become more active, the contributions of the specialist remain almost inaccessible. They could satisfy that curiosity, and ought to be made known. Since the publication of Edmond Faral's study in 1933, more than thirty years of research and discussion have passed; it is time the results were evaluated. The object of the present volume is to attempt this reassessment while recalling the particular merits of the work itself.

Medievalists are always attracted by the problem of origins and often are not primarily concerned with a literary examination of the *Chanson de Roland*. Hence the highly technical character of my first chapters — they may prove all the more confusing to the general reader since their results are sometimes inconclusive or negative. Fortunately the work itself compensates for all the fruitless attempts to explain its genesis, as I have tried to demonstrate in the second part of this study. My exactitude and enthusiasm have been the greater for the hope of reaching a large audience and thus serving the glory of a very great poet, probably one of the most remarkable in French literature.

Paris, 1967   Pierre Le Gentil

CONTENTS

ILLUSTRATIONS

(following p. 22)

Window from Strasbourg Cathedral (ca. 1200). Musée de l'Oeuvre Notre-Dame. Photo Giraudon.

Statues from Verona Cathedral (twelfth century). Photo Roubier.

Statue from Chartres Cathedral (twelfth-thirteenth century). Photo Roubier.

Tapestry from Bayeux (eleventh century). Photo Giraudon.

Miniature from the *Chanson d'Aspremont* (thirteenth century). British Museum.

Miniature from the *Grandes Chroniques de France* (fourteenth century). British Museum.

Illustration from the *Chroniques et Conquêtes de Charlemagne* (1458). Bibliothèque Royale de Belgique.

THE

Chanson de Roland

ONE · THE TEXT

People have been talking about Roland and his exploits for centuries, but the *chanson de geste* that immortalized him has been known only for slightly over a hundred years. The little-heard history of this precious text deserves to be told.

It is not particularly surprising that the men of the seventeenth and eighteenth centuries were not interested in knowing the authentic *Roland*, and that they were content to read Pulci, Boiardo, or Ariosto. The romantic nineteenth century, with its interest in early civilizations, proved far more attentive and demanding, and the first edition of the *Chanson de Roland* appeared in France in 1837. The *Cantar de mio Cid* had been known in Spain since 1799, but the task of studying it was left to the Austrian, Ferdinand Wolf. That study dates only from 1831.

The first edition of the *Roland* arrived late, but it was the work of a Frenchman. His name was Rolland Francisque-Michel; he was young — twenty-eight years old — and with this achievement marked the beginning of a long and brilliant career as a medievalist. The details are important in evaluating his work, for chance plays a greater part than merit in some discoveries.

Francisque-Michel was not the first to draw attention to the *Chanson de Roncevaux,* as it was called around 1830. In 1817 a manuscript of the poem had been reported to the Société des Antiquaires de France by a cousin of Alfred de Musset, and the maternal grandfather of the poet, Claude-Antoine Desherbiers, had promised to publish it. But the years went by. Finally, in circumstances that are unclear, a student at the Ecole Normale Supèrieure named Henri Monin decided to submit a "Dissertation sur le Roman de Roncevaux" to his professors. His thesis was immediately honored by being published, earning the praise of François Raynouard and the title of doctor for its author; this occurred over a period of several months during the year 1831–32. Monin used two manuscripts: the one that had already been reported and another, which belonged to the Bibliothèque Royale. A faithful account of historian Claude Fauriel's ideas, combined with a conscientious analysis of the texts, increased the interest of his work.

At this point Francisque-Michel intervened. In his *Examen critique de la dissertation de M. Monin,* which also appeared in 1832, he pointed out the existence of a third manuscript, almost unknown in France: the Oxford manuscript. He owed his information to an unlikely source, Chaucer's *Canterbury Tales* in the Thomas Tyrwhitt edition (1775–1778). Between two other brief references, the name of Turoldus had been transcribed for the first time since the Middle Ages, and this was enough to arouse Michel's curiosity. The only problem was to recover the precious volume. On the recommendation of Fauriel, Guizot agreed to send the young investigator to England under government auspices. He arrived in London in September 1833, stayed there at length to copy various texts, and at last, after pleading on several occasions for a renewal of funds, triumphantly wrote Louis-Jean-Nicolas Monmerqué on July 13, 1835: "I am writing you from Alfred's city, two steps away from the Bodleian, where I have just found . . . what? . . . Guess . . . the *Chanson de Roland!*"

The preparation of the edition took two years. They were well spent, for in addition to the exact reproduction of the Oxford text, Michel included a glossary and gave a complete description of all the known versions of the *Chanson*. But the appearance of his edition did not have the expected repercussions; the French did not understand the value of the treasure that had just been returned to them. Joseph Bédier has pointed out that two hundred copies of Francisque-Michel's edition satisfied the curiosity of scholarly Europe for more than thirteen years. Fortunately, things changed.

The first editor of the *Roland* realized that the Oxford text occupied a unique place within the manuscript tradition of the poem; after innumerable investigations and debates, this is still the prevailing opinion. A comparison of the various known versions of the *Roland* follows.

The Oxford manuscript — Digby 23 of the Bodleian Library at Oxford, designated by the letter *O* — is a text of 3,998 decasyllabics divided into 291 assonant strophes (*laisses*). It was most probably copied in England, and is written in Anglo-Norman dialect, but the original could well have had another source and other linguistic characteristics. Paleographic experts, summoning all their technical resources, place it in the second quarter of the twelfth century. Those who prefer evidence of the philological order arrive at essentially the same conclusion. The *O* manuscript is definitely superior in one basic and very concrete respect: its age. Despite the editorial alterations it contains here and there, however, it is not flawless. Faithful as the copyist seems to have been to his model, he is occasionally guilty of omissions or errors, some serious enough to render several passages entirely unintelligible. This fact suggests that admiration for the O manuscript should be tempered by caution.

The other manuscripts are much more recent, but it is not only because of their age that they are considered inferior. The first that should be mentioned is V^4, number IV of the French collection in the Library of San Marco in Venice, now numbered 225. It is written in that curious and artificial Italianized French that was long stylish among the singers of the *chansons de geste* beyond the Alps, and consists of 6,012 lines divided into 413 assonant strophes. Today its date is set as fourteenth-century. The same library owns a second version of the *Roland*, which comes from the collections of G. B. Recanati and had originally belonged to the Gonzague family. It is V^7, otherwise referred to as number VII of the French collection, now numbered 251. This copy seems to have been executed in Italy at the end of the thirteenth century; it contains 8,880 lines divided into rhymed strophes that are not assonant. Very similar to V^7 is a manuscript known as the Châteauroux, C or Ch. This text has 8,330 lines grouped into 452 rhymed strophes; it also comes from the Gonzague library but originally was part of the collection of Louis XVI at Versailles, from which it was acquired by the scholar Jean-Louis Bourdillon, who bequeathed it to the municipal library of Châteauroux, his native city. The C manuscript was copied in the thirteenth or fourteenth century, either in the Midi of France or in Italy.

There are three other manuscripts. The first is number 860 from the Bibliothèque Nationale, the P manuscript. It is the one that Henri Monin used, along with *C*, in 1832. The Paris text, which is damaged at the beginning, was copied in the thirteenth century and belonged to the Colbert library. It consists of 373 rhymed strophes, totaling 6,830 lines, and its language seems to reveal characteristics of Lorraine or Wallon. Manuscript 984 of the municipal library of Lyon (*L*) is fourteenth-century and doubtless comes from Burgundy or Franche-Comté. Unfortunately it is very incomplete: curiously bedecked with an Arthurian opening, the narrative begins at the moment when the battle of Roncevaux starts, stresses the death of Roland and Aude, and ignores the Baligant episode. It consists of only 2,933 lines, divided into 213 rhymed strophes. The *T* manuscript, R 3.32 of Trinity College Library at Cambridge, has two considerable lacunae; executed in western France at the very end of the fifteenth century, its 5,705 lines are divided into 355 rhymed strophes.

Under number 5,327 in the New French Acquisitions, the Bibliothèque Nationale has the two *Fragments Lorrains*, totaling 347 lines, which were discovered by Henri Michelant in the region of Metz around 1840. Several fragments of a lost manuscript, originally from the east and containing a total of 108 lines, constitute the *Fragments Lavergne*, so called because of their editor's name. French variations of the *Roland* also include the Provençal *Ronsasvals* and the *Galien*. The *Ronsasvals* is of an episodic nature and is limited to an account of the battle; it was composed in the fourteenth century and introduces both new characters and new themes. The *Galien* celebrates Oliver's son and seems to be a sort of synthesis of the *Pèlerinage de Charlemagne* and the *Roland* itself. Its editions are late fifteenth-century: one (the Cheltenham version) in verse, the others in prose. Two of these texts remained in hand-written form, while two were printed several times after 1500 and still circulated in the last century in cheap editions. Clearly the *Ronsasvals* and the *Galien* — and perhaps the Provençal *Roland à Saragosse* — can cast some light on the later developments of the Roland tradition.

The foreign versions of the *Chanson* have proved informative in other respects. The best known and undoubtedly the oldest, 9,094 lines in length, is the *Ruolandesliet* of the Bavarian priest Konrad. It was long supposed to be a product of the first half of the twelfth century, but was in fact composed around 1170. It later served as a model for Stricker's *Karl der Grosse* (around 1230) and the anonymous *Karl Mainet*. No less important than Konrad's work is Part VIII of the *Karlamagnussaga* in Norse prose, compiled between 1230 and 1250 by Robert the monk at the request of the Norwegian king Haakon Haakonsson, who was a great lover of French stories. Also noteworthy are the *Campeu Charlyamen* in Welsh prose and the verse fragments of the English *Song of Roland*, both of which date from the fifteenth century but could have used a much older French model. The Middle Dutch *Roelantslied*, probably one of the first landmarks of Netherland literature, is almost useless: the five existing fragments, completed by several verse passages from a more recent popular booklet, are difficult to classify and interpret. Still more mutilated is the thirteenth-century Castillian *Roncesvalles*, of which only a hundred lines remain. It introduces, and very adroitly at that, the character of Renaud de Montauban into Roland's ranks, which suggests that it has emended or imitated versions that were already substantially altered. Two Latin texts complete this list: the *Historia Karoli Magni et Rotholandi* of the pseudo-Turpin, in prose, and the anonymous *Carmen de prodicione Guenonis*, in verse. These two works are incontestably related to the French *Roland* in that all three are founded on a legendary, and not a historical, tradition. It is generally agreed that the date of the prose work of the pseudo-Turpin is about 1150, but there is considerable disagreement about the *Carmen;* some believe it to be extremely old, while others, who are probably right, find in it all the characteristics of a late work, around the second half of the thirteenth century.

It is important to distinguish between the assonant and the rhymed versions of these texts. Since the use of assonance is earlier than that of rhyme, the rhymed texts would presumably be more recent. We would thus connect the *O* and *V*⁴ versions, on one hand, and on the other the *C, V*⁷, *P, L,* and *T* versions as well as the *Fragments Lorrains* and the *Fragments Lavergne.* The rhymed versions have in common the fact that — aside from *L* — they are much longer than *O*. The transition from one form of versification to another cannot in itself account for this lengthening. It is the result of stylistic profusion and the introduction of new episodes, most notably in the second part of the narrative, after the capture of Saragossa, when Charles finally takes the road for home. A final visit to Roncevaux provides the pretext for scenes of mourning which recur, with the same emotional effect, at Saint-Jean-Pied-de-Port and Saint-Jean-de-Sordes. At this point Ganelon escapes from his guards, but is retaken after a chase and an exciting struggle. Then at Blaye, the death of Aude becomes a short story of melodramatic misfortune. Ganelon's judgment is augmented by a brutal scene — a debate among the barons, who have been asked to select the traitor's torture: one can imagine how they compete in originality and ferocity! There is no further need to point out the superiority of the assonant Chansons de Roland over the rhymed ones, of the early versions over the revisions in which the equilibrium has been upset and the effects sometimes clumsily exaggerated.

According to all the evidence, we must look to the *O* and *V*⁴ versions for the true *Chanson de Roland*. The real problem is to ascertain how much we should trust each of these two documents. Their superiority to the others has been demonstrated, but this excellence might well be only relative. *O* is far from perfect, and V^4 has certain peculiarities. After following a model exactly comparable to that of *O* in the first part, V^4 suddenly introduces an episode not found in any other version: Charlemagne's siege of Narbonne. And when it continues the narrative after this interpolation, it abandons the assonant model that was initially followed and joins the rhyming versions. Thus the only homogeneous copy we have of the assonant French *Roland* is, with its good qualities and its faults, the irreplaceable Oxford manuscript. We have to trust it, whether we like it or not. But do its merits eliminate the necessity of consulting the other versions in case of difficulty?

Bédier replied in categorical fashion to this question, asserting the "précellence" of the Bodleian text. According to him, its validity can be proved in almost every respect. Even when it is obviously faulty, nothing proves that the other versions come any closer to the original or reveal the exact content of that original.[1] Although the critics have finally rallied to this point of view, their acceptance is generally qualified: many are still unwilling to devote to the Oxford manuscript what might be called a religious respect. But when they do rebel and allow for a correction that Bédier would not countenance, they seldom reach the same conclusions. Perhaps these contradictions suggest that confidence is less hazardous than skepticism, but the fact remains that the Oxford text cannot be considered either the archetype of the *Chanson* or the direct and absolutely reliable copy of that archetype. All we can say is that, despite its imperfections, it offers the least deformed or the most authentic known

[1] For more detail, see the Bibliographical Note, on editions.

version of the first masterpiece of French literature, and it alone has the right to the title *La Chanson de Roland*.[2]

We must be content with this conclusion. Some readers will consider it only partially satisfactory, and certainly it cannot be completely so. Unfortunately, the rest of this volume will prove a serious disappointment to anyone who demands certainties or aspires to the absolute satisfaction of his curiosity.

[2] Henceforth when speaking of *La Chanson de Roland*, I shall be referring to the Oxford version.

TWO · THE EVENT

Reduced to its basic outline, the narrative of the *Chanson* centers on the heroic but ill-fated battle at Roncevaux in which the rear guard of the French army perishes, to the last man, at the hands of the Spanish Saracens. The commander is Roland, Charlemagne's nephew. With him are his wise companion Oliver and the valiant archbishop Turpin. Because Roland is so sure of his own valor and that of his men, he sounds the oliphant only when it is too late: the emperor finds only corpses on the battle-field. The enemy has fled at his approach. The ambush is the result of treason, plotted out of fear, spite, and hatred by Ganelon (Roland's stepfather), the pagan king Marsile, and his adviser Blancandrin. The first part of the poem describes the circum-stances, causes, and progress of this crime, which affects not only Roland but Charlemagne, the empire, and Christianity. The second part shows, in three episodes, how Roland's death is avenged. First, Marsile sees his army drowned in the waters of the Ebro. The emir Baligant, who, as head of the combined forces of Eastern Islam, has just joined the Spanish infidels, then perishes at the hand of the old emperor himself. Finally Ganelon is condemned after a trial that ends in a judicial duel, and then quartered, as is suitable for traitors of his ilk. This is not pure imagination. The poem is based on a historical event, though the discrepancy between the poetic and historical accounts is considerable.

What, then, do the Carolingian chronicles tell us, and how do the modern histories based on them describe the events at Roncevaux? The oldest related text, the *Annales Royales,* is contemporaneous with these events. It is limited to an explanation of the conditions under which Charlemagne crossed the Pyrenees to intervene in Spain at the request of a Saracen embassy. Not a single allusion is made to the battle at Roncevaux in the year 778. However, a revision of this chronicle, twenty or twenty-five years later, mentions that in 778 the emperor had the misfortune to see all his Spanish victories negated upon his return by an attack in which the Basques killed most of the French leaders, carried off the baggage, and disappeared completely unpunished into the mountain passes of the Pyrenees. We must wait for the *Vita Karoli* of Eginhard (770–840), written around 830, to find more specific details, and particularly to learn the names of the principal victims.

Whilst the war with the Saxons was being prosecuted constantly and almost continuously he [Charlemagne] placed garrisons at suitable places on the frontier, and attacked Spain with the largest military expedition that he could collect. He crossed the Pyrenees, received the surrender of

all the towns and fortresses that he attacked, and returned
with his army safe and sound except for a reverse which he
experienced through the treason of the Gascons on his return through the passes of the Pyrenees.

For while his army was marching in a long line, suiting
their formation to the character of the ground and the de-
files, the Gascons placed an ambuscade on the top of a
mountain — where the density and extent of the woods in
the neighborhood rendered it highly suitable for such a purpose — and then rushing down into the valley beneath threw
into disorder the last part of the baggage train and also the
rear-guard which acted as a protection to those in advance.

In the battle which followed the Gascons slew their opponents to the last man. Then they seized upon the baggage,
and under cover of the night, which was already falling,
they scattered with the utmost speed. The Gascons were
assisted in this feat by the lightness of their armor and the
character of the ground where the affair took place. In this
battle Eggihard, the surveyor of the royal table, Anselm,
the Count of the Palace, and Roland, Prefect of the Breton
frontier, were killed along with many others. Nor could this
assault be punished at once, for when the deed had been
done the enemy so completely disappeared that they left
behind them not so much as a rumor of their whereabouts.[1]

During the ninth century, many other annals continue or re-
capitulate this narrative. One of them, which is only ten years
later than the *Vita Karoli*, deserves special attention: the *Vita
Hludovici Imperatoris* whose anonymous author is often referred
to as the Astronome of Limoges. He evokes the Pyrenean defeat

[1] *Early Lives of Charlemagne, by Eginhard and the Monk of Saint Gall,*
trans. A. J. Grant (London, Chatto and Windus, 1922), pp. 19ff.

of 778 in a vague and pompous manner, but adds a bit of information that cannot but attract attention: "Those who were marching in the rear guard of the army were massacred in the mountains; as their names are so well known, I won't bother to mention them again." In other words, the battle at Roncevaux had so struck men's imaginations that, more than sixty years afterward, the names of the victims were still strong in their memories. Strangely enough, no text even mentions the name of the pass, although the precise date of the battle has been passed on to us by a strange document. It is the epitaph in Latin verse which can be found in the *fonds lat.* manuscript 4,841 at the Bibliothèque Nationale; it deals with the seneschal Eggihard, Roland's companion in misfortune. According to this account, the battle took place on the fifteenth of August, and Eggihard was buried in a church dedicated to St. Vincent — the location of which is not known.

Thus Roland became the hero of a *chanson de geste* which has made his name famous forever; Eggihard was the one to produce the document, but the poets were as uninterested in him as they were in Anselm, whose very existence would be unknown without the brief reference in the *Vita Karoli*. What different fortunes for men equally well known in their time, who died side by side, on the same day, in the same place! Turpin's presence is another surprise. He is certainly based on a historical figure, the archbishop of Reims (c. 753), but the real man died in either 789 or 794, at least ten years after Roncevaux. A fanciful and now discredited tradition has it that he was the author of the *Historia Karoli Magni et Rotholandi* — the *Chronicle of Turpin* — which was inserted in the *Liber Sancti Jacobi* around 1150.

Several important pieces of evidence have yet to be discussed: first, coins, minted in 781, which bear the name *Hrodlandus;* then, a charter that establishes the presence of a *Rothlandus*, who could well be our hero, in good standing among the *fidèles palatins* around 772. The narrative annals are always better at stimulating one's curiosity than satisfying it, but we shall now venture an interpretation. It is generally accepted that the battle of Roncevaux was not an ordinary struggle of the rear guard, no simple upset. It was obviously a catastrophe that was nearly fatal to the empire; official contemporary historiography, unable to pass over it completely in silence, made obvious efforts to limit its significance. And it is not easy to understand a battle in which, amidst general confusion, the great leaders perish to the last man at the hands of an adversary who goes unpunished. The magnitude and speed of Charlemagne's reprisals in Aquitaine the day after Roncevaux are significant. But if the emperor had to leave Spain, why did he not fear for the safety of his men in the rear? The curious conditions under which the Pyrenean campaign was decided upon and undertaken, at considerable expense, provide another problematical aspect. The Carolingian chroniclers themselves admit that Charlemagne decided to intervene on the peninsula at the request of the ambitious Saracen governor of Saragossa, Suleiman ben al-Arabi, who was in revolt against his master, the Omayyad emir of Cordova. It is difficult to say what he expected. Charlemagne appeared at Saragossa, where he thought the gates would open at a word from his ally, al-Arabi. Nothing of the sort happened. The city resisted, the siege dragged on; bad news from Saxony necessitated a hasty return, almost a forced march. On the way they encountered a city that refused them passage although it was Christian: Pamplona. The emperor razed it without mercy, then fell into the fatal ambush in which he came to know the "treachery of the Basques." But it is possible that the Basques were given considerable assistance by the Arabs. According to the historian ibn-al-Athir, the sons of al-Arabi succeeded in freeing their father, who had been the prisoner of

Charlemagne since the battle at Saragossa. Other witnesses report negotiations between the emperor and Abd-al-Rahman, adversary of al-Arabi.

These few clues do not provide a satisfactory explanation for the battle at Roncevaux, but they are enough for readers of the *Chanson de Roland,* to whom they suggest that between the event of 15 August 778 and the narrative of the Oxford manuscript, copied around 1150, there is both a considerable discrepancy and an obvious connection. The poem describes Charlemagne's expedition into Spain and the disastrous battle of the rear guard that marked the end of this expedition. It recalls one of the most famous victims of the ambush. But this is absolutely all that connects it to history. The rest — the essence, in our eyes — is legend and poetry.

How was the connection between the twelfth-century masterpiece and the eighth-century defeat perpetuated, and how did it acquire such artistic import in the process? The Carolingian chronicles are irrelevant, since the author of the *Roland* does not seem to have drawn his information from that source. Was he then inspired by a written or an oral legend? Did he use poems earlier than his own? What inventive gifts did he possess himself? We do not know if documents exist other than the annals which can be relied on to answer these questions. For all their searching, the critics have apparently not been able to find them, let alone make them speak clearly. But before we deal with this issue, we must try to solve the problem of chronology.

THREE · THE DATE AND
AUTHOR OF THE
OXFORD *ROLAND*

Everyone is agreed that the Oxford manuscript was probably executed in the second quarter of the twelfth century, but for lack of reference points it is more difficult to be specific about the date or location of the original poem. We are limited to deduction and cross-checking. What clues do exist are diverse, but their interpretation is always delicate; they barely allow us to go back any earlier than 1100–1080, or possibly, according to the critics who are most eager to prove the antiquity of the archetype, 1060. However, the *Ruolandesliet* by the priest Konrad, which paraphrases and sometimes even translates the Oxford *Roland* literally, can provide a *terminus ante quem* that is quite late if, as is now admitted, Konrad's work is no earlier than 1180. And if we consider a curious passage in the *Canso d'Antiocha* of Grégoire Béchada, the oldest circumstantial reference to our

Chanson would be between 1130 and 1142. There are other less characteristic or significant references and imitations to which we shall return. Basically the problem is to ascertain whether the *Chanson* was composed *before* or *after* the First Crusade, and whether we should still accept the conclusions advanced by Bédier in 1927, in his *Chanson de Roland commentée*.

Bédier doubtless understood that an investigation founded solely on linguistic elements, or on details of armament, costume, and custom, or even on ways of thinking and feeling, could only lead to very approximate results. Such an examination would place the *Roland*'s composition in a late eleventh-century atmosphere; in this way the outer limits can be defined. But, within this broad framework, how can we arrive at a specific date, in the strict sense of the word? Bédier ignored the allusions to the occupation of Jerusalem by the Infidels and to the sacred Lance, both of which are open to diverse interpretation, and first turned his attention to the words *Butentrot* and *mahomerie:* the first could be a reference to an episode of the First Crusade immediately before the battle of Dorylée (1 August 1097), which, according to the chroniclers, took place in the "Valley of Butentrot" in Cappadocia; the second could not have been used to mean *mosque* until after the first expedition to the East. Similarly, the word *Canelius* is used to describe the Canaanites, who were identified with the Saracens, and thus would seem to be drawn from the vocabulary of the first preachers of the holy war. It is equally significant that the *Roland* poet ranks Slavs, Hungarians, Bulgars, and Armenians among Baligant's battalions, and that the emir Baligant is inevitably reminiscent of the Fatimid caliph of Cairo, *amiratus Babyloniae,* who only came to be known at the battle of Ascalon, 12 August 1099. Finally, we must not forget that Charlemagne's army was full of priests and prelates, as were the armies of the Crusades, or that the poet stressed the tight solidarity uniting the entire world of Islam against Christianity. He would probably not have done so if he had written before a battle such as Antioch.

If the *Chanson* dates from the year 1098 at the earliest, as Bédier concludes, how much later than this might it be? Here his response is based on a passage from Raoul de Caen's *Gesta Tancredi* (1112–1118) and on a justly famous section from the *Gesta Regum Anglorum* (1125) of William of Malmesbury. Because these two authors refer to the *Roland,* he says, we can assume that the poem enjoyed a wide reputation after the *first years* of the twelfth century, and had been famous for some time: otherwise William of Malmesbury would hardly have dared say, when describing the preparations for the Battle of Hastings in 1066, "Tunc, cantilena Rolandi incohata, ut martium viri exemplum pugnaturos accenderet . . . praelium consertum" (Then, before the battle, the Song of Roland was chanted, so that the men might be encouraged by the martial example of the hero). Although Bédier did not pretend that his argument was flawless, he offered this conclusion: "The *Chanson de Roland,* composed after the Council of Clermont [1095], was famous in 1118, perhaps in 1112, and had already appeared when William of Malmesbury was still a very young man, that is, around 1100: we are thus led to place its appearance at the very beginning of the twelfth century or, at the earliest, the very end of the eleventh, let us say between 1098 and 1100." But he asked, with a final scruple, is there not "something disturbing in the very precision of such a result?"

His answer is still valuable, although it has been subject to constant discussion since 1927. Certain of Bédier's arguments are no longer acceptable, but others have replaced them. Opinion on the date of 1100 is certainly not unanimous; nor should it be considered as definitely established. The following discussion will not cover the details of the scholarly controversies, and it may not provide the means to form an opinion, but it will at least give a concrete idea of the difficulties that medievalists encounter when they examine problems of literary chronology. In a text like the *Chanson de Roland* it is hardly surprising that the slightest details of language, style, or vocabulary which might conceal an allusion to a contemporary scene have been systematically examined, line by line, word by word. The historians particularly seem to have rivaled one another in ingenuity, since they are persuaded, with good reason, that no writer could detach himself from his own time and would consequently react more or less openly to the events he witnessed. It would be dangerous to contest the validity of such an assertion, but the statement clearly entails risks.

Prosper Boissonnade responded by transforming the *Chanson de Roland* into a veritable *poème à clef:* a surprising result, no matter how generous the effort. No one would deny that the French expeditions into Spain in the eleventh and early twelfth centuries were related to the development, if not the origin, of the Roncevaux legend. But it is surely farfetched to maintain that Gaston de Béarn, Rotrou du Perche, Sánchez Rámirez, Alphonse le Batailleur, and even Robert de Normandie are all revived, whether simplified or synthesized, in the Roland of the poem. The geographic identifications that Boissonnade proposes are of course seductive, and it is interesting that they focus our attention not only on the pilgrims' route of Saint-Jacques-de-Compostelle, but also on the region of Saragossa and the high valley of the Ebro, which was precisely the location of the eleventh-century Franco-Spanish "crusades." But does the fact that Tudela appeared in the history of these crusades only in 1087 and was not captured by Rotrou du Perche until 1114 mean that the *Chanson* — which attributes the conquest of this city to Roland — was necessarily written after this date? Was it then composed after the capture of Saragossa in 1118, or after the victories at Cutanda and Daroca between 1120 and 1124, because the memory of these glorious events made it easier to imagine Charlemagne's twofold victory over both Marsile and Baligant after the massacre at Roncevaux? Albert Pauphilet was also interested in the Franco-Spanish crusades and, surprised at not finding a reference in the *Roland* to the famous siege of Barbastro in 1064, decided that the date of composition must be in the vicinity of 1060. Such discrepancies give rise to skepticism.

The relative disrepute into which Boissonnade's book has fallen has not discouraged the search for allusions that may be revealing though they are unrelated to geography or history. Henri Grégoire sees reflected in the *Chanson*, and particularly the second part, the experiences of Robert Guiscard in Epirus between 1081 and 1085. The Butentrot discussed by Bédier would then be Butrinto in Epirus, where the Normans victoriously encountered the Byzantine army in 1081: a memorable episode that would explain why Podandos in Cappadocia was transformed into Butentrot during the First Crusade — though all these Butentrots are perhaps more simply explained as a reference to the legend of the traitor Judas, which has been linked to the Butrinto of Epirus. In any case, Grégoire feels that the expression *Terre de Bire*, which figures in the last strophe of the *Roland*, refers to the province of Epirus itself. As for the Canelius mentioned by Bédier, they would not be Canaanites, but inhabitants of Kanina, which is near the Jericho in Epirus. Further, the toponym *Imphe* would be another name for Dyrrachium (Durazzo), where, in another significant coincidence, a Norman garrison was blockaded in 1085 during a return offensive by Baselius. Could the *Chanson de Roland* then have been written to speed the recruitment of reinforcements to rescue the surrounded post? Grégoire thinks so, just as he believes it possible to link the emir Baligant to Georges Paleologue, since with a little good will the name *Baligant* could look like a French adaptation of *Palaiologos*. Thus it follows that the composition of the *Roland* could only have been before the First Crusade.

Emile Mireaux goes much further. Since his proposed correspondences cover an extensive period of time, he feels compelled to postulate the existence of several Chansons de Roland. He has decided that the original poem was dominated by a strong Carolingian loyalty, or rather by a nostalgic protestation against the recent brutal accession of the Capetian dynasty. So much for the year 1000. This first poem would have been followed, around 1085, by a version that was revised and augmented by Italo-Norman inspiration. Charlemagne's conquests in the *Chanson* would correspond to those of both William the Conqueror and Robert Guiscard in Sicily or in the Balkans. Finally, and I simplify, he ends with the Anglo-Angevin Oxford edition, which, around 1158, would have sought to focus attention on certain aspirations of Henry II, who had become the rival of the king of France. But let us delay no longer over opinions that, despite their abundant evidence, have gathered few disciples.

There are other arguments of some interest which, for the sake of completeness, should be mentioned. There are details in the *Roland* text that are striking because of their visibly archaic nature. Charlemagne solemnly entrusts a bow to Roland before the battle (line 767), but in the eleventh century the bow was no more than a hunting weapon: the idea of making it a symbol of command must be quite old. Still more striking is the *Chanson*'s description of the boundaries of France: Saint-Michel-du-Péril and Xanten on one hand, Besançon and Wissant on the other. This is the region over which Charles the Simple reigned after his coronation in 911. Thus the true France, that of the *Francs*

de France in the poet's words, would be the Francia of the tenth
century; a France which, acccording to Ferdinand Lot, had not
yet been reduced to the regions around Paris and Orléans by
the ambition of the Foulques, the Thébauts, the Eudes, and the
Herberts, who deprived it of Angers, Blois, Chartres, Troyes,
and Meaux; a France whose capital was no longer Aix and was
not yet Paris, but, as mentioned once in the text, was Laon.
Similarly, critical interest has recently been drawn to Ganelon's
trial. The procedure and verdict do not correspond to eleventh-
century custom, but these departures should probably not be
thought of as mere archaisms since they may have more to do
with imagination and artistic creation than with judicial tradition.
Why should a poet who is writing at the end of the eleventh
century not try to evoke the distant time in which his narrative
takes place?

In any case, it is clear how the problem of unity grows out
of the effort to date the Oxford *Roland*. Contradictions and discrepancies could be partially explained by the fact that the
poem is the result of successive efforts and contains, along with
extremely old elements, some very recent additions or interpolations. This chapter began with a question on the date of the
Oxford manuscript. What should our conclusion be? Along with
the majority of the specialists, notably Maurice Delbouille, one
of the more recent *Roland* scholars, we can consider 1100 as
the most probable date. Here is why.

Although the author of the *Roland* makes no direct allusion
to the pilgrimage of Saint-Jacques and the Franco-Spanish crusades, it is clear that he has both specific and vague ideas about
Pyrenean and peninsular geography. The man who attributed the
conquest of all Spain to Charlemagne is not acting as a historian
of either the 778 expedition or those of the eleventh century.
He is acting as a poet who is free to combine truth and reality

Supposed portrait of Charlemagne, between Roland and Oliver. Stained-glass window in the Cathedral of Strasbourg (ca. 1200).

(left) *Statues in the Cathedral of Verona* (*twelfth century*).

Supposed statue of Roland, carrying a shield decorated with fleurs-de-lis. South doorway, the Cathedral of Chartres (*twelfth-thirteenth century*).

Charge of the Norman cavalry. The Bayeux Tapestry (eleventh century), also known as the Tapestry of Queen Mathilde and a treasure of the Cathedral.

Roland saves Charlemagne by killing the pagan Eaumont. Miniature from the Chanson d'Aspremont (thirteenth century).

Siege of a city by Charlemagne and his barons. Miniature from the Grandes Chroniques de France (fourteenth century).

Comment rolant le noble combatant mozu
en la tresdouloureuse iournee de ranicheuaulx

Pour ce que listoire des quatre filz
hemon nest point a mettre aucase
ceste presente Je men deporte et re

The death of Roland, from the Chroniques et Conquêtes de Charlemagne *(1458).*

with the suggestions of his fantasy and imagination. But the ideal by which he is inspired, the conflict he recalls, and the meaning he gives it, all suggest that he lived in the memorable years that knew Christianity while Urban II was pope, particularly since it is the First Crusade to the East more than any other previous or contemporary historical event that dominates his thought and gives flight to his inspiration. Such unity of tone reigns that, even if it is only the completion of earlier efforts, we must consider the work homogeneous. We should be able to locate it specifically in time and place, in relation to the *most recent* of the indications that can serve to establish a *terminus post quem.*

Although few and unobtrusive, such clues exist, and they confirm our previous impression. In listing both England and southern Italy among Charlemagne's most notable conquests, and in referring to Saint Peter's poll tax, the author of the *Roland* could well be thinking of William the Conqueror and Robert Guiscard. His familiarity with the Ports of Cize, as well as of the regions of Valtierra and Tudela, suggests that he might have in mind the battles that made these places famous toward the end of the eleventh century. By placing a relic, part of the sacred Lance, in the handle of Charles's sword, he could be referring to the miraculous "revelation" which, in 1098, comforted the Crusaders who were besieged in Antioch by Corbaran. The Spanish critics have noted that in using the word *taburs* and in speaking as he does of *chameaux*, he could be echoing a celebrated episode of the Spanish *reconquista*, the battle of Zalaca, undertaken and lost in 1086 by Alphonse VI, suzerain of the Cid: in fact the new sound of the tabors and the unprecedented use of camels in this battle were the principal causes of the Christian defeat at the hands of Almoravides. Further evidence includes certain coins (*besans esmerés*) and a linguistic peculiarity studied by Delbouille involving the abbreviation of unstressed personal pronouns. We always end up in the last years of the eleventh century, in the ambiance of the First Crusade, as Bédier thought.

Finally there is the question of the author. There is no need to know his name — or even his native region or social condition — in order to appreciate his masterpiece and his genius. However, the last line (4,002) of the *Chanson,* so often cited and so diversely interpreted, makes it impossible to accept without question the fact that we do not know:

Ci falt la geste que Turoldus declinet.

Although it appears only in the Oxford manuscript, there is no reason to doubt the authenticity of this *explicit.* The question is how to interpret the words *geste* and *declinet.* Bédier felt that in the poem the word *geste* generally refers to a source, probably Latin, which the author invokes; he was also struck by the Latin form *Turoldus.* His tentative translation would be: "Here ends the narrative which Turoldus recounts (sets forth, develops) in his chronicle." It was a common custom among medieval writers to include a reflection on the nature and character of their work in a brief epilogue. But here, rather than taking advantage of the opportunity to speak of *himself,* as was usual, the poet would have been invoking in Turoldus his *model.*

Bédier's opinion has at least the merit of illustrating the variety of meanings that can be attributed to this passage. *Geste* could be understood to mean either the *Chanson* or the text it claims to recall. *Declinet,* which is in the present tense, could mean *expresses, transcribes, declaims,* or *puts into verse.* In other words, Turoldus could be considered the original author ("Here ends the *geste,* the narrative-source, that Turoldus writes"), or the author of the *Chanson*'s source (as Bédier suggested), or a scribe ("the tale, the narrative, that Turoldus transcribes"), or a jongleur charged with its performance ("the poem that Turoldus declaims"). Still another interpretation is possible: "Here ends the poem, for Turoldus has not the strength to continue."

Are all these hypotheses equally plausible? As we have seen, Bédier tried to choose. But Delbouille has noted that we are dealing with an *explicit*, and since the *explicits* of this genre are in general a means for the authors to sign their works, it is natural *a priori* to regard Turoldus as the poet's name. In this case the word *geste* could have the general meaning of *tale*, or *adventure*, and not that of *authoritative text*, which it normally has in the verses of the *Roland;* in any case this latter meaning really depends on the fact that it is always qualified, as in expressions like *geste Francor* and *ancienne geste*, or in the passage that validates the alleged narrative written at Laon by Saint Gilles (not Turoldus), who was a witness of the battle. Thus we are led to venture the following interpretation: "Here ends Turoldus' account, that is, the tale that provides the subject of his poem." *Declinet* would then be used in its usual sense, which is well expressed by the present tense. The Latin form of *Turoldus* is not really so surprising, especially in association with the school word *declinet*. There are many other Latinisms in the poem, particularly in Roland's last prayer. Our first impression would then be correct: the author of the Oxford poem, that powerful spirit to whom we owe the first masterpiece of French literature, may well have been called Turoldus.

Must we be content with a possible name? The critics could not help looking further. Having established that Turolduses (or Thorolds) "abounded" almost exclusively in England and Normandy between 1050 and 1150, and that the text of the Oxford manuscript is written in Anglo-Norman, they risked some enticing identifications. Some dreamed of the Turoldus of Fécamp who was made abbot of Malmesbury by Willam the Conqueror immediately after his victory; others of the Turoldus who was bishop of Bayeux from 1097 to 1107 and was still living in retirement at Bec in 1127; others of the Turoldus who was abbot of Coulombs near Chartres and who died in 1131. Boissonnade finally found a Turoldus who fitted into his thesis, not just in Spain but even in Tudela! But of what value are the titles of these various candidates? One would have to be either very shrewd or very presumptuous to answer this question; we have to admit that we do not know. We are not even certain that the scribe of the Oxford version had a model that was already written in Anglo-Norman. Like so many others, he must have been capable of Normanizing a French text. What is certain is that if his name was Turoldus, and if he was therefore either Norman or of Norman origin, the author of the Oxford *Roland* did not reveal any deep Norman prejudices. It is enough to see the role he gives to the "Franks of France" to understand that, if he is related to the descendants of the Vikings, his ideal transcends regionalism to attain to a real nationalism.

Again, a name and a biography are important, but most significant is genius. It is in the *Roland* itself, and nowhere else, that we shall find the most exact and complete image of its creator. This is not only to recognize the obvious value of the poem; it is also to advance a hypothesis of its genesis, which in turn means becoming involved in the debate about origins.

FOUR · BEFORE THE
OXFORD *ROLAND*

Before confronting the theories that claim to explain the genesis of medieval epics, we should describe the evidence on which the arguments will be based. This inventory ought to provide the answer to at least one question: should the appearance of the *Chanson de Roland* around 1100 be considered a sudden event or one long in preparation?

A survey of tenth- or eleventh-century works in *langue d'oïl* may be quickly made. Their relation to the *Chanson de Roland* is indirect, since they are still quite rough artistically and are of an exclusively didactic character. Although the combination of heroism and sanctity occasionally appears in the hagiographic accounts as well as in the epic narratives, the differences between an Alexis and a Roland are still considerable. But is there any trace of what might be called a fermentation of the oral epic between the eighth and eleventh centuries? Evidence has been produced which is of considerable interest if we do not try to attribute a greater significance to it than it deserves. First, there is the testimony of the monk of Saint-Gall, at the end of the ninth century, which alludes to the stories of the old soldiers; in the same period, the Poeta Saxo mentions vernacular songs celebrating famous people; a line in the Latin manuscript 5,354 of the Bibliothèque Nationale, from around 1050, also notes this fact. Then there is a passage in the *Vita Sancti Faronis* of Hildegaire, written before 875, which provides what some people think is still better: the Latin translation of an authentic romance *cantilène*. We must not overestimate this evidence, however. Short poems were doubtless sung, on the occasion of great events or in honor of certain people, which involved refrains performed by a choir or along with the steps of a dance. But nothing proves that these poems were in content or in tone of a truly epic character, or that we should look to them not only for the germ of future epics, but also for the very elements which would make a coherent unit of the *chansons de geste*. Furthermore, it is now assumed that the Latin verses of Hildegaire are a forgery, a pious hoax intended to enhance through the time-honored technique of panegyric the glory of the saint worshiped at Meaux. Still, if we must abandon the effort to reconstruct the alleged romance model for these verses, the fact remains that their author would probably not have bothered to invent them if his effort had *not* been likely to delude his readers, who must have been used to hearing "rustic songs" dedicated to contemporary celebrities. But that the beginnings of the epic actually lie here is probably unlikely and certainly open to discussion.

The *Fragment de la Haye* should also be discussed in an examination of the origins of the *chansons de geste*, and its significance rated in connection with the preceding evidence. It is generally considered to be the Latin prose version of a poem, also in Latin, which recounts with mythological allusions and much artifice the siege of a pagan city; on this occasion it glorifies characters whose names are reminiscent of certain heroes of the geste of Guillaume d'Orange. The paleographers claim that these three parchment leaves were written by three students between 980 and 1030. Does this mean we can assume that an embryonic epic about Guillaume's lineage already existed at the beginning of the eleventh century? It seems unlikely that this epic would have first been composed in the vernacular, then translated into Latin hexameters, in order finally to assume the form of Latin prose, though certain battle descriptions and intentional repetitions are similar to the future *Chansons* and might suggest this. Perhaps the *Fragment de la Haye* is relevant only to the history of the Latin epic in the Middle Ages. But in that case a comparison between this Latin epic and the *chansons de geste* seems inevitable.

In fact, those who pursue this comparison will be disappointed. The Latin works that can be grouped with the *Fragment de la Haye* are artificial and scholarly. Although they are inspired by the most authentic Virgilian tradition, they generally reveal less of an epic sense than a skill at flattery and rhetorical games. Since they are panegyrics inspired by contemporary realities, they do not even treat the same subjects as the French songs, and if the songs sometimes recall the Latin works in technique or style, they are still far from producing the same sound or striving for the same effects. Then we have the *Waltharius*, a truly curious text whose theme has been compared, despite the strained analogies, to that of the *Roland* and of the Spanish romance of Galiferos — after having been linked to the most ancient German traditions. It deals with a certain Walter of Aquitaine, who is a hostage at the court of Atilla; he escapes, carrying off the royal treasure as well as his fiancée, who was also the prisoner of the king of the Huns. Their flight, which occasionally verges on the ridiculous, involves romantic, folkloric, and warlike episodes. Latinists, Germanists, French and Spanish romanticists have, alternately or simultaneously, claimed as their own this strange poem, which one would hesitate to call a true epic. Furthermore, it is still not known whether it is ninth- or tenth-century, nor who the author is. According to the most recent German analyses, it could well be no more than the imaginings of a clerk, an isolated work without repercussions, relying on a simple imitation of Statius. We can hardly attribute to it a rich heritage, or even recognize in its pretentious and mediocre verse any significant merit as evidence. It would prove far more valuable to look elsewhere and give up the examination of the Latin epic. The most we can learn from such poets as Ermold le Noir, who told of Louis le Pieux and the capture of Barcelona, is that at the start of the ninth century such figures as Charlemagne or Guillaume de Gellone were beginning to take on a legendary stature in clerical writings.

Of course it would be vastly preferable to show that Roland himself also benefited from a progressive poetic idealization — but here disappointments are again in store. We must wait until the first years of the twelfth century to see serious writers unequivocally evoke the memorable battle and its most famous victim. Thus the allusions of Hughes de Fleury (1109), of Raoul de Caen (1112–1118), of Raoul le Tourtier (1109), of the monk of Silos (1110–1115), of William of Malmesbury (1125), or of Orderic Vital (1135) — to list only the oldest ones — could quite simply reflect the success and recent fame of the Oxford *Chanson* itself. William of Malmesbury does claim that the *catilena Rolandi* he mentions was sung among the Norman ranks, in 1066, before the Battle of Hastings. How does he know, since he was not there? This reference probably should not be accepted at face value, although a text from about 1074 might have suggested to William what he ultimately expanded upon.

Along the same line of thought, Bédier stressed the fact that between 1050 and 1120 the abbey of Saint-Jean-de-Sordes, on the route from Bordeaux to the Pyrenees, produced some documents falsely attributed to Charlemagne: the monks of the abbey, to enhance the prestige of their establishment, consulted the Carolingian annals and made their contemporary forgeries correspond to the expedition of 778, which was conveniently reminiscent of the eleventh-century Spanish crusades. Bédier also felt it was possible to prove that the monuments at Roncevaux demonstrated the existence of local legends about Charlemagne and Roland in that region before 1100. Actually these monuments cannot be accurately dated; the chronological evidence we have about them goes no earlier than 1106. That is the year in which the Crux Caroli, erected at the Ports of Cize, is first mentioned in a papal bull; except for a passage in the *Roland* — to which we shall return — Roland's tomb at Blaye is not mentioned until 1109, by Hugues de Fleury, and it is only between 1127 and 1132 that references appear to the "rock of Roland," to the Capella Caroli Magni, or to the Hôpital des Pèlerins at Roncevaux. Of course it is entirely possible that earlier, strictly local legends about this rock of Roland were suddenly revived, giving rise after 1080 to monuments of increasing importance. But it is possible that the *Roland* itself was finally responsible for all these monuments. The risk of confusing cause and effect is clearly great.

Despite these uncertainties, it seems sure that a legend about Roland existed on the *via Jacobitana*, and more specifically at Roncevaux, by the end of the eleventh century or, at the latest, the beginning of the twelfth. Furthermore it would seem that the systematic exploitation of this legend in connection with the pilgrimage of Saint-Jacques and the French expeditions to Spain began only at this time. Perhaps old memories were revived after a long silence as a result of the success of the *Chanson de Roland* itself. At any rate, this was the opinion to which, until recently, most people cautiously subscribed. Some new facts now seem to have reopened the debate. Primarily they concern Oliver's name and its association with Roland's in a number of recently discovered documents.

Albert Pauphilet was one of the first to draw attention to the character of Oliver. Since he is not mentioned in the chronicles, it seems most probable that he was a product of the poet's imagination, created out of diverse elements to illustrate or revitalize the poetic theme of warrior companionship. In any case, it clearly was a masterful writer who attributed antithetical qualities to these inseparable friends, one the brother and the other the fiancé of the beautiful Aude, and took full advantage of this antithesis which governs the drama at Roncevaux and makes it so moving. Now, if at a certain moment two brothers were respectively named Roland and Oliver by their parents, and if at the same moment this was not an isolated fact, we would be in a position to draw a very important conclusion. These names probably could not have been chosen and connected except in recollection of a famous literary work in which the epic pair, Roland and Oliver, held a central position. This work must have been a *Chanson de Roland* written in a Romance language; otherwise the wide circulation that must be ascribed to it cannot be easily explained. But which *Chanson de Roland*? Was it the Oxford version or another, older one?

The answer depends on the date of the documents under discussion.

These documents are numerous, but they are not always of indisputable authenticity or value. To date, the oldest we have comes from Brioude and goes back to the years 1011–1031; it implies a baptism which occurred around 1010 at the latest, and we would therefore be led to suppose that an epic narrative about Roland had been in existence since about 1000. According to Rita Lejeune, this conclusion would be confirmed by a curious text of Dudon de Saint-Quentin, written between 1015 and 1020. It describes a battle, preceded by a peace mission, during which a certain "Francisci agminis signifer nomine Rotlandus," after having rebuked one of his companions — the ambassador, in fact — for belligerence, perishes as a victim of his own temerity. The analogy with the *Chanson de Roland* is apparent. However, the Brioude document has been challenged, since it is not known whether the Oliverius and Rotlandus mentioned there were actually brothers or merely close relatives. A similar uncertainty eliminates a document from Lérins that goes back to the years 1026–1069. Another, from Saint-Victor de Marseille and dating from 1055, is now considered, with or without reason, to be a forgery.

On the other hand, we have three admissible documents that link the names from Saint-Aubin d'Angers, Béziers, and Saint-Pé-de-Générès in Béarn, whose respective dates are 1082–1106, 1091, and 1096. Obviously they do not permit us to propose the existence of a poem about Roland before 1060. Certain critics even go so far as to argue that people in the eleventh century never took literature into consideration when selecting the names of their children. Relying on documents where the signatures of Roland and Oliver are apparently unrelated, they maintain that the association of these names, which seems elsewhere to be so conclusive, is fortuitous. They point out that, in any case, this association might indicate the success of a *legend* as well as that of an actual *epic text*. More serious is the fact that the names are associated in a different way after the date of these documents. Until 1100, the sequence always appears as Oliver-Roland. It was only later that priority was given to Roland, suggesting the influence of a genuine *Chanson de Roland*. It is fair to assume that something happened at the end of the eleventh century which altered previous custom and led to the elder instead of the younger being named Roland, when that position had previously been reserved for Oliver. This event could well have been the appearance of the Oxford *Roland*. Paul Aebischer, who supports this point of view, assumes that the previous custom had to do with an early (hypothetical) *Gérard de Viane* in which Oliver might have had precedence over Roland. If there was a flourishing of epic at the beginning of the eleventh century which suggested to certain parents this choice of names among all the glorious possibilities, it was quite different from that reflected by the extant poems of a hundred years later.

Theories on the origin and diffusion of Oliver's name are perplexing. In the Midi and Catalonia, the form *Olivarius-Oliverius* seems to have replaced the ancient *Oliva-Oliba*, but this substitution could have been due to influences from the north. What sort of influences? One might more happily reply that they were literary influences if it were certain that *Olivarius-Oliverius* did not appear on any of the old charts except in association with *Rotlandus-Rollandus*. In this case we could favor the argument which notes that the olive tree was traditionally the symbol of wisdom, and maintains that the Roland-Oliver couple was thought up by some clerk to illustrate the classical and biblical topos opposing *fortitudo* and *sapientia* or recommending their simultaneous practice. Nothing could be less certain, however; according to Aebischer, *Olivarius* could easily have been taken from the contemporary "anthroponymic lexicon" without any initial relation to *Rollandus,* especially since the olive tree is more a symbol of peace than of wisdom. This debate seemed promising at the beginning, but it has added to the confusion rather than alleviating it.

Perhaps we have to look no farther than a discovery of the 1950s made in Spain by Dámaso Alonso, pertaining to a new document, the *Nota Emilianense* — written in rather defective Latin about the battle of Roncevaux, a subject that to this point none of the annals has mentioned. On a sheet torn about a century ago from the Emilianense 39 manuscript at the Real Academia de la Historia, page 245 recto, this passage appears:

> In era dcccxvi [Spanish era, beginning 38 years before the Christian era] uenit Carlus rex ad Cesaragusta. In his diebus habuit duodecim neptis; unusquisque habeat tria milia equitum cum loricis suis, nomina ex his Rolande, Bertlane, Oggero spata curta, Ghigelmo alcorbitanas, Olibero, et episcopo domini Torpini. Et unusquisque singulos menses serbiebat ad regem cum solicis suis . . . Contigit ut regem cum suis ostis pausabit in Cesaragusta; post aliquantulum temporis, suis dederunt consilium ut munera acciperet multa, ne a famis periret exercitum, sed ad propriam rediret. Quod factum est . . . Deinde placuit ad regem pro salutem hominum exercituum ut Rolande belligerator fortis cum suis posterum ueniret . . . At ubi exercitum portum de Sicera transiret, in Rozaballes a gentibus Sarrazenorum fuit Rolande occiso.

The text can be translated thus:

> In the year 778 King Charles came to Saragossa; at that time he had twelve nephews (or grandsons?) with him, and

each of them had three thousand armed horsemen with him; among them were Roland, Bertrand, Ogier of the Short Sword, Guillaume of the Hooked Nose (*alcorbitanas* could be a corruption of *al corb nes* and of *curbi naso*), Oliver, and the bishop Turpin. Each one, with his followers, served the king one month of each year. It so happened that the king stopped at Saragossa with his army. After a short time he was counseled by his men to accept a number of gifts so that the army might not perish from hunger and could return to their homeland. This was done. The king then decided that, for the safety of the men of the army, the courageous warrior Roland should remain with the rear guard. But when the army traversed the Port of Cize, at Roncevaux, Roland was killed by the Saracens.

The examination of textual details, particularly concerning date and authenticity, has certainly not been exhausted. According to the experts consulted by Alonso, manuscript 39 — originally from San Millán de la Cogolla — on which the note was transcribed, belongs to the tenth century. It does not necessarily follow that the *note*, isolated among texts with which it has no connection, is equally old, but since it is written in Visigothic printing, it could not be much more recent. Because it seems to be in the same hand that copied other documents at San Millán between 1048 and 1070, particularly in 1065, Alonso and Menéndez Pidal suggest the third quarter of the eleventh century, at the latest, as its date. They cannot be too highly commended for resisting the temptation to propose an earlier date. Thus we are inclined to adopt their conclusion that fairly circumstantial accounts of the battle at Roncevaux were known in Spain before the Oxford *Roland*, at least as early as the third quarter of the eleventh century.

The *Nota Emilianense*, admittedly, does not breathe a word about the warrior companionship between Roland and Oliver, and, as Pidal mentions, it seems to be unaware of Ganelon's treason. But it is familiar with the theme of the twelve peers, who are presented in a particular manner: Ogier is in a position of prominence and, more strangely, so are Bertrand and Guillaume. The note knew the date of the battle, probably from a chronicle, and better still, though from another source, knew the place in which it was fought. Thus there certainly was a considerable flourishing of epic elements a good half-century before the composition of the *Roland*. We may be tempted to believe that this activity had already produced wonderful *poems* that deserve to be called *chansons de geste;* but we should rather assume that, however brilliant these efforts were, they had to undergo significant change before reaching the same form and quality that characterize and recommend the extant texts.

In a debate of such importance, no source of information should be neglected. The review of evidence is still not complete: the details relevant to the various versions must now be discussed.

Among the texts that deal with Roland, the *Pseudo-Turpin* has been of particular interest to critics, as has the *Guide des Pèlerins de Saint-Jacques*. In our oldest manuscript, the *Codex Calixtinus,* these two texts comprise parts four and five of a huge collection, the *Liber Sancti Jacobi.* The first three parts include an anthology of liturgical pieces honoring the apostle, a list of his miracles, an account of his preachings in Spain, his martyrdom in Palestine, and the transfer of his ashes to Iria in Galicia. The *Pseudo-Turpin* is the *Historia Karoli Magni et Rotholandi* presented as if it were the work of the archbishop Turpin. It first recounts how Charlemagne discovered the saint's tomb and organized his cult at Compostela after a victorious expedition in which he completely overran

Spain and destroyed all the idols, except the Colossus of Cadiz. The episode at Roncevaux occurs at the end of a second campaign, which was provoked by the arrival in Spain of the African Agolant. Charles is again victorious and is about to return to France. With Ganelon acting as interpreter, he orders the pagans of Saragossa, Marsirus and Baligandus, to have themselves baptized or pay tribute. Ganelon reveals himself to be a treacherous messenger, while wine and women lead the French to commit the gravest excesses, for which they will soon be punished.

It is now that Roland, *nepos* of Charles and count of both LeMans and Blaye (or is it Blois?), is called upon to take command of the 20,000-man rear guard. Marsirus attacks them in two successive waves. During the second engagement he is killed by Roland, but the French are decimated. Twice Roland blows his horn to rally the last survivors around him, and his final effort is to break the oliphant. Grievously wounded, fainting with thirst, he dismounts and bids a fond farewell to Durendal, which he tries in vain to crush against a rock. After a long prayer he dies, attended by Thierry. Meanwhile Baudouin rejoins the main army and tells them of the massacre. The sound of the horn has also alerted them, and Turpin, who was celebrating Mass in the Val Carlos, has learned of the disaster through a vision that revealed Roland's entrance into Paradise. The emperor then returns to Roncevaux, and takes Saragossa. After a duel between Pinabel and Thierry by which he is convicted of treason, Ganelon is quartered on the spot. The bodies of the heroes are finally embalmed and transported to Blaye and Arles. Charles returns to Aix, where he soon dies in the midst of signs and miracles. Thanks to a new vision, the archbishop Turpin witnesses Charlemagne's judgment, which is effected before God by the intervention of a headless Galician, evidently Saint James.

The *Guide des Pèlerins* lists the four routes commonly used by

the followers of the apostle, which join into a single route beyond
Puente-la-Reina and lead to Compostela. On the way, it describes
the Val Carlos, the Crux Caroli at the Ports of Cize, the hospice
and church at Roncevaux. Finally it mentions the tomb of Roland
at Blaye and the oliphant, worshiped as a relic at Saint-Seurin de
Bordeaux.

Thanks to a contemporary witness, we know that the *Codex
Calixtinus* was already preserved in the archives of the cathedral at
Compostela in 1173. Since a revised version of the *Pseudo-Turpin*
had been used in a 1165 *Vita Karoli*, this date can be generally considered as the *terminus ante quem*. On the other hand, since one of
the miracles in Book II dates from 1139 and the *Guide* reports the
death in 1137 of Louis le Gros, the *terminus post quem* could be
set around 1140. However, one allusion in the *Pseudo-Turpin* permits us to focus on the year 1145. In this year the huge statue at
Cadiz was overturned, but, according to the text, that was the only
pagan idol to escape Charlemagne's religious demolition. It is thus
agreed that the *Liber* in five parts was finished around 1150. But
the real question is whether it should be considered an integral
whole. Bédier, followed by Horrent, has defended the thesis of its
unity, persuaded that a single purpose — the glorification of the
apostle James and his sanctuary — dominates the entire work.

Numerous critics, on the contrary, notably Meredith Jones and
Pierre David, assert that the *Liber* is comprised of elements that
are too disparate to be the work of a single author. Various details, particularly the rather glaring contradictions between the first
three parts and the last two, and even between the *Pseudo-Turpin*
and the *Guide*, seem to prove them right. As a result, the date
1150 pertains only to the final collection, which was probably the
effort of Aimeric Picaud: a letter at the end of the *Codex*, alleg-
edly from Innocent III, grants him a kind of safe passage to bear
the precious anthology from Flanders to Compostela. Of course

such a hypothesis does not necessarily mean that the *Pseudo-Turpin* or the *Guide* is significantly older. In fact, Bédier's adversaries date the texts around 1140–1145 and 1130, respectively. Incidentally, it is clear that the *Liber* as a whole, in content as well as in spirit, reveals a character more French than Compostelian: It is the French pilgrims in whom the author of the *Guide* is primarily interested. The author of the *Pseudo-Turpin*, who so curiously rescues the archbishop from the massacre for the purpose of hiding behind him, is generally far less concerned with the cult of Saint James than with the epic legends themselves.

From this thorny discussion we can conclude that, in any case, the *Pseudo-Turpin* and the *Guide*, works of French inspiration, are later than the Oxford *Roland*. Did they know and use this *Roland*, or did they have access to other sources? If so, were these hypothetical sources older than the *Roland* itself, and what were they like? Could the author of the *Roland* have used them as well? There is no need to point out how convenient it would be to have a clear answer to these questions. But it may not be possible to be as specific in answering them as we would like. Opinions on this score are sharply divided. After closely examining the texts and considering their differences, some critics have concluded that the *Pseudo-Turpin* and the *Guide* used only the French poem. Others, stressing the differences, try to find through them evidence of a tradition that precedes the poem. The *Pseudo-Turpin* does not mention Blancandrin's mission or the Baligant episode. It does include Ganelon's treachery, although it tries to present the disaster as a punishment for grave excesses. Moreover, it associates Baligandus, whose model we almost surely know, with Marsirus. At the end of the battle a new character, Baudouin, becomes the object of our sympathetic attention, at Oliver's expense, and Thierry conveniently escapes the massacre to recount what happened — but these surprising changes do not necessarily mean that we ought to propose divergent traditions. In attributing his narrative to Turpin, which seems to be an idea of his own invention, the author puts himself in the position of having to save a witness and give a definite character to his narrative. It is perfectly possible to maintain that many elements in the *Pseudo-Turpin* make sense only if they are seen as echoes of the Oxford *Roland,* where they existed for a reason forgotten by the transposer in his eagerness to condense the drama or to incorporate the style of an austere, edifying chronicle.

In this respect Jules Horrent's argument, for example, seems very convincing. But the opposite efforts of André Burger and Paul Aebisher are also very impressive. From a minute examination of foreign versions, particularly the Norse *Karlamagnussaga,* Aebischer has concluded that the Roland tradition is multiple; that, in addition to the Oxford version, it could have taken other parallel or contrasting forms. Burger believed he could prove that the author of the *Pseudo-Turpin* was familiar with the Oxford *Roland,* but that the author of the *Guide des Pèlerins* knew neither of these texts. The similarities that connect all three would be the result of a single common source, a Latin poem, a *Passio Rotholandi,* more hagiographic than epic, of which many almost unaltered meters can be reconstructed from the *Guide* and the *Pseudo-Turpin.* The reconstruction of these hexameters is somewhat hypothetical; yet it is probable that if the Oxford *Roland* was greatly exploited and imitated, it was neither the unique and complete model nor a creation independent of any source, Latin or otherwise.

The problem is to be more affirmative. Aebischer's evidence is elusive and Burger's suggested connections are highly debatable, or at least debated. Several years ago an effort was made to revaluate and clarify these arguments in light of the *Carmen de prodicione Guenonis.* But E. R. Curtis' work makes it difficult to cite this text, which must now be considered a typical example of thirteenth-century manners and taste. It is surely more reasonable to look at it as a very free abridgment of previous versions — even rhymed ones — than as a lingering example of some unknown primitive state of the Roland legend, before the addition of the Blancandrin and Baligant episodes. What is true of the *Pseudo-Turpin* or the *Carmen* seems also to apply to other reputedly archaic versions, primarily the *Fragments Néerlandais*. It is impossible to find a primitive *Roland* through these versions. Instead, as Horrent and his teacher Delbouille have succeeded in persuading us, they all seem to proceed more or less directly from the same tradition as the Oxford *Roland*.

While continuing the search for external clarification, we must return to an examination of the *Roland* text itself, in the hope of finding answers that these other texts do not help to provide. The aspects of the text that are relevant to the problem of chronology have been discussed. Others, which have long been noted, offer hints as to its sources or predecessors. On several occasions the poet refers to what he calls the *ancienne geste*, the *Geste Francor*. In strophe 155 he writes: "Thus it is reported by the geste and by him who was on this battlefield, the baron Saint Gilles, for whom God does miracles and made the charter in the church of Laon. Whoever does not know this much understands very little." There is no doubt that in the various examples the word *geste* alludes to a written work that would lend the authority and credence of a precedent. But it is not impossible that this work was invented for the needs of the moment. Knowing medieval customs, we cannot but consider this possibility, and the allusion to the baron Saint Gilles, who actually lived two centuries before the battle, is also suspicious. Bédier, however, concluded that "there was a book, doubtless written in Latin, which told of the war in Spain and whose author pretended to be Saint Gilles:

earlier than the *Pseudo-Turpin*, this chronicle of the pseudo-saint Gilles was known by the author of the *Chanson de Roland*." Such a hypothesis has now been confirmed by the studies and discoveries discussed above: the Roland-Oliver link, the *Nota Emilianense*, and the remarks of Burger and Aebischer. Unfortunately, if texts did exist before the Oxford *Roland*, it is extremely difficult to describe them, and references to a *Geste Francor* or a *Geste of the pseudo-Saint Gilles* cannot solve the dilemma. This is the essence of the problem. Obviously our poet did not invent everything, and it would be interesting to know the exact degree of elaboration attained by the material that he, in turn, exploited.

His material was not provided solely by written texts. Bédier has very rightly pointed to passages in the poem that refer to the tombs at Blaye and the relic at Saint-Seurin de Bordeaux. Here are two passages:

> (l.3685) Charles came to Bordeaux, the city . . .
> Upon the alter of the baron Saint Seurin he put
> the oliphant full of gold and coins. The pilgrims
> who go there see it . . .

> (l.3689) To Blaye he took his nephew and Oliver
> his noble companion, and the archbishop who was
> wise and brave. In white coffins he had the lords
> placed, in Saint Romain lie the barons . . .

It would have been difficult for the man who wrote these lines to have created such details from nothing. He had either seen these precious monuments or else knew about them because everyone around him spoke of them. If they existed merely in his imagination, he would hardly have called upon the very people to whom he was writing, the pilgrims of Saint James, as his witnesses. On the route to Roncevaux, at Blaye, at Bordeaux, and probably elsewhere, stories about monuments or relics, whether real or not, evoked in the author's time the battle of 15 August 778. They became known to him by word of mouth, and he took full advantage of them. But exactly what did they tell him? Another question, perhaps hypercritical, arises here. If the Oxford copy is not the archetype, perhaps the passages just quoted are recent interpolations. And speaking of interpolations, it is surely possible that the legends they reflect were created by the success of the archetype itself. In other words, there is a small but real risk here, as in the discussion about the structures at Roncevaux, of confusing cause with effect. Relics do not necessarily create the legends that explain them; it is equally possible that they arise after the fact to explain the legend. If, then, a split horn is preserved in Saint-Seurin de Bordeaux, it could be because the memorable lines of a great poet had already described Roland's death and the summons of his oliphant.

This doubt about the authenticity of the Oxford text naturally leads us to examine what Horrent, among others, has called its deficiencies. Peculiarities exist in the general order of this *Roland* and in the arrangement of certain of its episodes which could pass as weaknesses. They are especially noticeable because they are rare, and because there are occasional discrepancies between the "précellent" manuscript and the other versions, though they seem to be connected to the same tradition. It should be understood that there is no question of contesting the superiority of the Bodleian manuscript, which remains the finest example of this tradition. But if the manuscript and the model it copied only represent a step in an already long and complex literary development, then these deficiencies might provide an idea of either close or distant antecedents to the oldest and most beautiful *Chanson de Roland* that we know. And if the *Oxford* version was preceded by one or several chansons, can we discover their scheme or essentials?

The first area of criticism deals with Blancandrin's mission and Ganelon's behavior when he is delegated by Roland and then confronts Marsile in the pagan camp. When Roland utters the phrase that is to initiate the drama — "Let it be Ganelon, my stepfather" — the strophes in the Oxford manuscript are numbered 20–26, while in the other versions they appear in the following order: 20^a, 24, 23, 20^b, 21, 22, 25, and 26. Whereas in the *Oxford* version Ganelon's rage and anxiety are voiced immediately after Roland's unexpected suggestion, the expression of his anger in the other versions is much less abrupt and comes only after Charlemagne has acted on his nephew's advice, changing it into a decision and an order. It can thus be argued that in the Oxford text Ganelon's reaction to this frightening mission is premature, for Charles has not yet officially charged him with it. Roland speaks at line 279, and Charlemagne does not grant his approval until line 321. Further, by revealing his anger so precipitously, Ganelon takes on a belligerent quality that contradicts the genuine attributes of pride and courage recognized in him by the poet. And after proclaiming Marsile's good faith and supporting his peace offers before the French, it is irrational for Ganelon to react as he does when he sees that he has been designated to bear to Saragossa the decision he has just defended against the supporters of war. Here is another surprise: it is quite natural for Ganelon to reveal his spite toward Roland while talking with Blancandrin on the road to Saragossa. But when he reaches Marsile's camp, why does he assume a gratuitously provocative attitude that expressly contradicts the mission with which he has been charged?

Then there is Charlemagne's note to Marsile which is, in principle, meant to be conciliatory but, in fact, adopts a threatening tone. First it recalls the tragic precedent of Basan and Basile, who were also sent as ambassadors to Marsile and massacred by him, and then demands as an additional guarantee the delivery of the Caliph as hostage. Charles is using language that could endanger the negotiations and leave his messenger in a critical position. This is, in an irrational sense, perhaps enough to justify any treason. Blancandrin, far from letting his king know of Ganelon's secret inclinations from the start, only intervenes when Ganelon's remarks have touched off a dangerous quarrel. Had Ganelon been killed in this brawl, it would have meant the end of all plans for ambush and revenge. A final inconsistency: Blancandrin is completely ignored in the conclusion of the narrative, although at the beginning of the *Chanson* he occupies a primary position and seems destined to play a central role. We must ask whether the preliminaries of the battle in the Oxford version were not superimposed on a simpler tale, more clearly and logically constructed. Can we reconstruct this early version?

Some critics have not hesitated to omit everything about Blancandrin and his embassy from this hypothetical *Chanson de Roland*. It should be pointed out to them that the *Pseudo-Turpin* and the *Carmen* are not as conveniently oblivious as they might think to this prologue which unfolds the drama. The greatest objection to their argument is that, without Blancandrin's peace mission, it would be impossible to understand how Charlemagne, conqueror of all Spain except Saragossa, could have conceived of returning to France with as treacherous and formidable an adversary as Marsile at his back. An arrangement involving substantial guarantees must have been proposed to him by Marsile, who was anxious to avoid his own defeat. Such a transaction would presuppose an exchange of ambassadors. Without Blancandrin's mission, the betrayal itself, which is the only possible explanation for the ambush at Roncevaux, is not easily understood. Ganelon only thinks about revenge at first; in order to make an actual agreement with the enemy, he must be given the opportunity, and the peace conference provides just that. But a few confidences exchanged with Blancandrin are not enough. He must be provocative and insulting if he wants to awaken Marsile's bellicose spirit and turn it against Roland; although he counts on Blancandrin's intervention, his personal danger is great. It is certainly possible to insist, as Bédier does, on the authenticity of the prologue in the Oxford *Roland*. The good reasons we have for agreeing will seem better still when we examine the unity of the poem and can fully appreciate its solid structure from beginning to end.

The Oxford version might be accused of having changed the original order both within the prologue and elsewhere. A good example of this kind of limited revision would be in the strophes discussed above, 20 through 26. But the Oxford text is, finally, quite defensible in this particularly suggestive case; its order is as psychologically realistic as the alternative would be. In the passionate debate that divides Charlemagne's council into supporters and adversaries of peace, it is natural that Ganelon, hearing himself named by Roland, should consider his assignment established. He immediately realizes the reasons that make it inevitable, and also Roland's motives, heavy with hostile implications, in suggesting it when the emperor has just indignantly refused to endanger the twelve peers. It is hardly surprising that, without waiting for Charles' intervention, he should give free vent to the mixed emotions churning in his breast, or that he should think he is being ignominiously treated when he suddenly realizes the dangers of the negotiation he has himself advocated, one to which, he thinks, they are all eager to expose him. It is also natural that he should then call Roland to direct account and challenge him, and that Charlemagne, surprised and troubled by this hostile outbreak, should remain silent before sanctioning the choice and conferring the insignia of his mission on Ganelon. Here again a more complex study of the situation and characters will reveal the admirable solidarity of the Oxford text.

The text is not always perfect, however. In a few cases there seems to be either a lacuna or an inversion of several verses. It has been noted, for example, that the pagan Margariz alone escapes the first encounter at Roncevaux. By making him survive, the poet probably intended to have him announce the defeat of the advance guard to Marsile. If the Oxford copy is imprecise here, the rival versions tell us that this is what is expected. Everything suggests that we are dealing with one of those omissions that are so common to scribes. Further, the relative confusion that reigns in the narration of the second part of the battle is striking. In particular, the fight between Turpin and the pagan Abisme, Marsile's standard-bearer, seems out of place. The two strophes that describe it (lines 1467–1509) come too early in the Oxford text. In other versions they are located at the end of a series of single combats, at the moment when Marsile himself advances on the field of battle. Turpin's exploit thus comes at the perfect time to rekindle the courage of the French, who have already been decimated, and Roland's rousing eulogy of the archbishop acquires a timeliness that it lacks in the Oxford manuscript. A lacuna could still explain the inadequate description of Marsile's escape in the Oxford *Roland,* and some sort of rearrangement might have affected strophes 83–85, where Roland lists his reasons for not recalling the emperor without establishing any connection between them. Strophes 125 and 126 suggest a similar conclusion. In none of these cases is there positive evidence of what could actually be called rewriting: we are probably dealing with minor accidents that do not exceed the limits of common scribal initiative or error. It would then seem more impossible than ever to discover through the Oxford poem anything but the model of which it is a relatively faithful copy. At no point can we see taking its place the significantly different picture of an original *Chanson de Roland,* distinct and indisputable.

There is a final and important objection to be dealt with. If the authenticity of the Blancandrin episode has, probably wrongly, been contested, that of the Baligant episode has been argued even more. Of course, in one sense Baligant's defeat might seem unnecessary, since Marsile has already been conquered. He alone is implicated in the events at Roncevaux, which is and must remain the center of the drama. Must Roland, who is finally the sole master of the field of battle, be revenged twice? Charles only needs to make the enemy pay for the loss of his men; he does not at all have to repair a situation of actual defeat or erase any shame. Besides, the Baligant episode, which faces Charles with a task disproportionate to all that precedes it, places his character in such prominence that the figure of Roland suffers unfortunately by comparison: it has been said with some reason that the Baligant episode actually transforms the *Chanson de Roland* into a *Chanson de Charlemagne* and that as a result the general equilibrium of the work is disturbed.

There are problems of presentation and style as well as atmosphere. Up to the drowning of Marsile's troops in the waters of the Ebro, nothing allows us to foresee a sudden and substantial renewal of the action. Seven years ago Marsile, at bay, had asked the all-powerful emir of Babylon for aid. That the emir required this long period of time to assemble all the peoples of Heathendom is credible, but how unrealistic and awkward that he should arrive, unannounced, at the very moment when Marsile, believing himself reduced to his last forces, has just gambled everything! The Baligant episode seems to be dominated by a particularly abstract and ideological conception of the Crusade, which has systematic recourse to the marvelous and the supernatural. Surely the beginning of the work is more concrete and human, its style less ambitious and tainted with rhetoric, more firm and sure.

The importance of these alleged contrasts, which could easily be countered by listing the many symmetries that exist, should not be exaggerated. We must remember that the appearance of the amazing emir has the effect of elevating the conflict to mythic proportions and that the style must sustain this change by reaching for the sublime as best it can. But this is not the real point. Whether we like it or not, the Crusade as a sacred and eternal mission of Christianity, surpassing the level of individuals, has dominated the poet's thought from the beginning of the poem. For him the drama at Roncevaux is certainly caused by human passions, but he judges them in terms of whether they help or harm the Crusade. Thus Roland's rashness, his *démesure*, is transformed into an ideal sacrifice worthy of glorification. But Ganelon's desire to avenge himself for a personal injury leads him to commit the most unpardonable of crimes. This is why the proceedings at Aix are so solemn, and the verdict so cruel, so ignominious. It is also why the death of Marsile, merely the king of Saragossa, is not enough to avenge the ambush at Roncevaux: all of Islam must be overthrown in the person of Baligant, the only adversary worthy of Charlemagne. Thus is revealed the sanctity of the cause and the invincibility of the Faith for whose defense Roland, refusing all compromise, spends the rich treasure of his heroism. From such a perspective it is clear that the Baligant episode could not be deleted from the *Roland* without destroying its equilibrium and contravening the author's intentions.

Again, the Oxford version holds its own. The infrequent deficiencies of the manuscript can only help us to know more about the original state of this version, altered here and there by copyists. To try to go beyond this archetype and find a *Chanson de Roland* that was not familiar with Blancandrin and Baligant, or that presented the drama differently, is a dangerous and probably chimerical enterprise. This is not to say that a hypothetical *Chanson de Roland*, which some people fruitlessly persist in trying to reconstruct, did not exist — but given the present state of our knowledge, it is beyond our reach. Since internal analysis of the available texts produces no results, the authorial references to sources and outside works mentioned at the beginning of this chapter must be considered with all the more attention. Of course they provide only clues, but these clues, which incidentally contradict one another, are extremely valuable.

First, they confirm the belief that sound logic suggests: a work like the *Chanson de Roland* could not have been created from nothing, even by an unparalleled genius; its author, whatever his merits might have been, profited by earlier efforts involving both the language and the themes that he himself was to exploit so remarkably. We would certainly like to be able to assess the extent and nature of these efforts. Apparently they were numerous and diverse. Those records from the second half of the eleventh century or earlier which reveal the frequent association of the names Roland and Oliver within the same family suggest the existence at this time of a literary work, in French or Provençal, idealizing their friendship. Allusions within the poem to the tombs at Blaye or the oliphant at Bordeaux are strong evidence of the formation of early oral legends along the pilgrim routes in France and Spain.

On the other hand, references to a *Geste Francor* and a *Geste of the pseudo-Saint Gilles* suggest Latin sources, a possibility that is also substantiated by Burger's work. It is quite possible that the author of the *Roland* used either the hexameters reconstructed by Burger from the *Pseudo-Turpin* and the *Guide* or, more likely, the poem from which they originated — whether or not it should be called *Passio Rotholandi*. Skeptics will at least recognize that the author could have used similar models. The *Nota Emilianense*, like the *Fragment de la Haye*, offers a truly curious confirmation of these various proposals. It places us in a clerical atmosphere where people express themselves in Latin, but the proper names it mentions are based on romance models. Its material is not limited to the Roland legend, since it is familiar with Ogier and Guillaume. Its description of Charlemagne's peers and its relative silence on Ganelon's treason link it to traditions that are slightly different, probably older than the one we know. Behind it, then, we glimpse a vast romance network. The possibility tempts us to look beyond the innovations of the Oxford poem for other numerous and complex ones, whether literary or popular, which might have been introduced over a fairly long period of time beyond the borders of France.

All this certainly extends the range of possible conditions under which the *Chanson de Roland* might have been composed. But there is a great lapse between 15 August 778 — the battle of Roncevaux — and the first half of the eleventh century, beyond which none of the available documents allows us to go. We should like to understand the formation of the epic legends, the men, the times, and the surroundings from which they evolved, the circumstances that favored their fruition and determined their success. We should like to know the form these legends might have taken in the course of their development — oral, written, Latin, French, or Provençal — and even more, when they became the object of literary elaboration, when they began to provide inspiration for poets and for what poets, when and by what stages they became real *chansons de geste*. Neither the *Nota Emilianense*, nor the eleventh-century records, nor allusions, nor the deficiencies of the Oxford text itself can provide a direct answer to these questions. We are just as badly informed about Ogier le Danois, Guillaume d'Orange, and Girard de Roussillon. The genesis of our medieval epics, particularly the *Roland*, remains hypothetical. This is not to say that arguments on the subject should cease. For over a century there has probably been too much discussion, since we now find that we have reached an impasse; but recent research and discoveries, however modest, may allow the debate to be usefully reopened. We must at least keep on asking although, in the end, it may seem that the hour of truth has still not arrived.

FIVE · THE *ROLAND* AND

THE ORIGINS OF

MEDIEVAL EPIC

It cannot be repeated too often that the discussion we are about to undertake has been dominated from its inception by a fact both glaring and mysterious: several centuries separate the event of 15 August 778 and the oldest version of the *Chanson de Roland* that we know. The connection between the reality of the event and the description in the poem is evident, but the difference is immense. Although the most recent research and discoveries tend to support the period around 1100 as the date of composition of the Oxford *Roland,* they still offer no precise and indisputable idea of the nature of the Roland legend before the second half of the eleventh century. No reliable document fills the gap, which presents as great an obstacle today as it ever did. Under these conditions no opinion, no matter how old, can be considered *a priori* as outdated.

Obviously the theories of romantic criticism have fallen into disrepute, and today it should be recognized that the mystique that inspired them no doubt cloaked a somewhat nostalgic interest. In our time no one would dare to assert that, before there were artistic rules and conventions, the original epic, "a direct and inevitable expression of nature," arose from a spontaneous overflow of the popular spirit at a moment when History and Poetry converged. No one claims any longer that the richness of effect achieved by the epic can be explained by the simplicity or naiveté of the methods it uses. To avoid the confusion that the concept of *popular poetry* can produce, it should be enough to say that it was not the mass of the people who, in one unanimous effort, composed the original epic songs; they were created by authors acting as anonymous spokesmen for the community. If so, we may have reason to believe that romanticism is not dead. In any case, not everything about romanticism should be scornfully rejected. By controlling the ambitious and fantastic generalizations imported from beyond the Rhine in Fauriel's time, Gaston Paris was able to offer a coherent theory of the *Roland*'s origin. He maintained that the consciousness of a new national character had gradually emerged in the wake of the racial mixtures produced by the Great Invasions. This phenomenon was accompanied by a rich poetic fermentation, and the results, reflecting national reactions to contemporary events, were lyric in form and epic in subject: short songs, fragmentary and impassioned, called *cantilènes*. When united and organized around a central theme or character so as to form long, continuous narratives, they became the *chansons de geste*. From the tenth to the twelfth century, then, the chansons used material that had been gathered between the eighth century and the end of the tenth. Thus no direct continuity between the event and the poem was apparent, and in this way both the durability of the memory and the profound changes it underwent are explained.

This hypothesis is easily applied to the *Roland*. The day after the battle, unknown poets who were full of fresh emotion, and perhaps themselves witnesses of the drama, sought to console Roland's companions by celebrating his unhappy but heroic fate. These short *cantilènes*, which appealed to the imagination and to the emotions, were transmitted orally from generation to generation and helped to create and maintain, along with the historical annals, an increasingly rich and evocative legendary tradition. They were constantly renewed and augmented, and soon made way for episodic poems devoted, for example, to the capture of the Nobles, the death of Basan and Basile, the siege of Carcassonne. Thus, bit by bit, a vast body of material evolved from which a final effort of organization and synthesis produced the form we know today, made famous by the various extant versions of the *Chanson de Roland*.

All theory aside, critics in Gaston Paris' time were clearly faced with an immense task: that of connecting, as far as possible, each medieval epic with the actual event of which it might be the more or less distant echo. It is undeniable that the work of the eminent philologist and his followers was extremely useful in this respect, and certainly they amassed a number of valuable documents and parallels. But because of the historical nature of their research, and the immense gap that often separates the chansons from history, the men of this generation were sometimes fatally led to accept questionable identifications and worse, in a difficult case, to mix themes or names — a process still known as epic transference. There is little reason to connect a narrative with one event rather than another when the similarities are only very approximate. And how can one prove that one character has been stripped of an authentic exploit while another, more fortunate, hero has had a number of adventures added to those he actually experienced? To see *cantilènes* everywhere, always to consider the existing works as more or less harmonious collections of initially independent pieces, is to incur the risk, on the smallest pretext and on the basis of arbitrarily magnified evidence, of breaking up texts that could have been created as a single, though perhaps imperfect, effort. The stocktaking in Chapter Four has perhaps shown that the nature and contents of the *cantilènes*, if their existence could be proved, are impossible to define for want of precise examples or allusions. A typical argument on this subject was directed against Gaston Paris by the Italian Pio Rajna; he was a romantic but, persuaded of both the German character and the great age of the *chansons de geste*, felt obliged to place the appearance of the first great medieval epics in the middle of the Merovingian era.

These remarks will explain the lively antiromantic reaction at the beginning of the century, of which Joseph Bédier was the champion. According to him, the French epic has only the loosest connection with history; it is based on *poetic themes* rather than *historical recollections*. The real characters and events that the epic evokes have been profoundly altered, or have become unrecognizable. Further, the culture, manners, and aspirations expressed reflect the period of the Crusades and of feudalism, not the Carolingian era in which the narratives occur. Texts and documents offer nothing to bridge the interval separating the eighth from the eleventh century, which would probably not be the case if these centuries had been the setting for any significant literary activity. And what is true today certainly applied in the time of the *chansons de geste*. It is a craft to make a book, as it is to make a table. Let us not speak of collective creation or of inspired crowds. We must look for an author and for the personal initiative, the excellence, and the faults that the word implies. Whether we like it or not, the decisive moment in the creation of a work of art is when the poet interprets the material at his disposal and organizes it with a particular end in view. The great *chansons de geste* are explained, above all, by a free and sovereign act of will. Each one is the gratuitous gift of a poet.

This does not necessarily mean that the material on which these chansons are based is insignificant. Bédier is careful not to disregard it completely. Despite the long period of silence, it would be difficult to claim that there was absolutely no connection between the poem and the event. Bédier believes that in the eleventh century there were pilgrimage routes; on these routes, sanctuaries; and in these sanctuaries, monks. Local and religious legends, linked either with the monuments or with regional disputes and organized to varying degrees, grew up along these routes. They were preserved in the sanctuaries and maintained by the monks for propaganda purposes. Through them, the memories were perpetuated even as they were transformed. Thanks to such favorable conditions as the Crusades or the eleventh-century cultural renewal, the jongleurs and the monks revived them, the latter offering their ill-assorted scholarly information, the former their imagination, cleverness, and occasionally talent or even genius. Thus the legendary material was organized and the phenomenon of literary creation occurred. Thanks to a productive collaboration that encouraged the most original impulses, the first chansons were born. Though he named his great work *Les Légendes épiques,* Bédier ended by praising the role of the poets and affirming that, like all masterpieces, the medieval epics begin and end in themselves.

It is not surprising that Bédier's ideas enjoyed a brilliant success from the beginning of the century up to recent years. To be aware of the exceptional artistic quality of the Oxford *Roland* is enough to see in it a masterpiece that is primarily explained by the genius of its author. When the ideal that inspired the poem is also considered, it is quite evident that the *Roland* could well be the product of a single period, that of the First Crusade. However little there is to be found in the great expanse of secular silence preceding its appearance — a silence that, with all its efforts, contemporary criticism has so ill succeeded in penetrating — it is still difficult to reject the idea of the routes leading to Roncevaux and Compostela. If we trust the official chronicles, it seems we would have the best chance of discovering the hypothetical *Geste of the pseudo-Saint Gilles* in a monastery along these routes. The richest source of legendary material about 15 August 778 would surely be found at Blaye where the white tombs of the battle's victims can be seen, at Bordeaux where a broken oliphant is preserved, and at Roncevaux itself, beside the rock of Roland. By 1100 there must have been more than enough in the tales of the monks, guardians of such marvelous relics and propagandists for both pilgrimage and crusade, to fire the imagination of a great poet.

Of course the originality and the age of the relics and monuments that Bédier cites are open to discussion. Further, the Oxford *Roland* does not make the slightest allusion to the route of Saint-Jacques or to the sanctuary at Compostela. Finally, an attempt to describe the exact process by which the monks and jongleurs joined efforts and managed to create a genre such as the *chanson de geste* might prove quite difficult. Clearly these problems are the basis for the fairly widespread opposition today to Bédier's doctrines. But we should point out that, though the author of *Les Légendes épiques* did not deviate from his own path, certain of his followers upset the balance of his tempting explanation. Thus, in an incisive and penetrating book that dealt with Bédier's disciples, the Italian critic Italo Siciliano could describe Faral as "pure," Boissonnade as "false orthodox," and Pauphilet as "false heretic." In any case, it is certain that Bédier's work has given rise to important research in the field of medieval Latin literature. This research may not justify the theories with which some have crowned it, but it does not deserve the discredit to which it is sometimes overzealously exposed. It ought to be discussed here.

We should recall that the high Middle Ages produced a fair body of literature of an epic-narrative character in Latin verse. Since it was fed by Virgilian memories, and generally adopted a eulogistic style, this kind of literature was admirably suited to maintain a taste for heroic theme and style among the clerks. It is difficult to avoid connecting it with the French *chansons de geste*. Bédier, who believed in the collaboration between monks and jongleurs, was the first to admit the debt of a work such as the *Roland* to clerical culture, particularly in the area of technique, though he asked that these scholarly influences not be overestimated. Curtius' remarkable work suggests that Bédier was right. Curtius underlines the frequency in the first landmarks of romance literature of certain Greco-Latin topoi — by which he means conventional rhetorical figures or themes that had become inescapable commonplaces. However, he is also aware that the tone and movement of the French and Spanish epics are highly original. His point of view eventually aligns itself with that of Bédier and confers a new value upon it. Other critics have not hesitated to go further. We remember Burger, who thought he had found the vestiges of a *Passio Rotholandi* in the prose of the *Pseudo-Turpin* and the *Guide des Pèlerins*. If we compare this discovery with the allusions in the *Roland* itself to the *Geste Francor* or to the *Geste of the pseudo-Saint Gilles*, then recall the *Fragment de la Haye* and the *Nota Emilianense*, and finally consider the presence of so many classical topoi in the Oxford text, we might be tempted to maintain that this text had nothing but Latin and scholarly sources. But if we succumb to this temptation, we must make the author a clerk and not a jongleur. And if the jongleur-monk collaboration is to be taken as Bédier's central assertion, then his thesis fails here. It is ironic, in any case, to see the author of *Les Légendes épiques* incur the same criticism he made of others: for Burger does not hesitate to say that to give the primary role of the poet to a popular singer and to reduce the monk to the position of catalyst is to be "romantic" all over again.

Let us return to medieval Latin literature and attempt to assess the influences on it. Clearly it is a continuation of a classical Latin tradition, but above all it is at the service of Christianity and the liturgy and hence grants an important place to music, which it perfected and made into a highly refined art. But it also placed this music within the grasp of a vast public whose participation in divine worship was desirable. Now our *chansons de geste*, in which a single assonance bound the lines into irregular strophes, or *laisses*, were sung. The musicologists think that there was a connection between this singing and that of the Church. Gennrich connects the *laisse* to the litany, which repeats the same melodic phrase indefinitely. Jacques Chailley thinks that the *chansons de geste* were originally chanted in a slightly less monotonous manner, like that in which the services of worship were read: thus their performance would have involved the use of melody-types for intonation, development, and conclusion. Since we have no early specimen of a notated strophe, this can only be a hypothesis, but there are two pieces of evidence that support it: the very form of the word *laisse*, which corresponds to the Latin, *lectiones*, and the music meant for the little epic couplets in the fine text of *Aucassin et Nicolette*. The services also included a sort of commentary in the form of tropes. These tropes were the point of departure for liturgical drama, but they might also have been developed in other forms such as the lives of the saints, which are so similar in certain respects to the *chansons de geste*. Finally, the mysterious AOI that appears in the margin of so many strophes in the Oxford text could well be a survival of an old refrain related to the *alleluia* or of a liturgical element adapted to epic declamation. Whether or not these various assertions are justified, the fact remains that the *chansons de geste* owe something, and perhaps a great deal, to the liturgy. Yet this clerical contribution, which is essentially technical, by no means denies the role of the jongleurs. Indeed, having played a large part in the diffusion of saints' stories in the vernacular, they were in a perfect position to adapt the various methods of religious singing to the demands of profane poetry, both epic and lyric. To succeed in these transpositions, a little cleverness sufficed and the jongleurs had more than enough. The public had little chance of remaining uninvolved at a time when divine worship held such an important place in daily life.

We have seen how the "Latinists" perpetuated Bédier's work in some respects, and this is even more true of the "liturgists." They allow us to look at the respective roles of monk, jongleur, and poet almost as Bédier does. But we cannot be satisfied with an impression. Before we can pass judgment on Bédier's ideas and evaluate the criticism about them, we must try to estimate their current validity. Nowhere is this subject better presented than in A. Viscardi's *Letterature d'oc e d'oïl* (1952). Here, in substance, is the argument of his essay.

The classical tradition was perpetuated in medieval Latin literature and progressively enriched by the contribution of Christian spirituality. At the same time, a new social order was established, dominated by feudalism. Under the influence of these various forces, a change took place over a period of several centuries. The principal craftsmen of future syntheses would be the clerks, the scholars; they were guardians of the cultural patrimony of the past but also active and influential members of chivalric society, whose ideals they sought to define and direct. Through their efforts, both in the atmosphere of the seigneurial courts and in the methods of instruction in the schools, the moral content and style of the lyric, epic, and romantic genres gradually increased. Next to this intellectual elite, which was so closely bound to the aristocracy, the jongleurs at first played a secondary role; but soon they were used to spread the clerical works intended for the secular public. Even the liturgy made use of the jongleurs, who kept in mind its methods and technique as they helped to elevate the Romance dialects. Soon it was no longer enough for them to be admitted to cultivated circles where they enlarged their repertoires and were rewarded for their skill as performers. As they became more confident, they too began writing.

At first this convergence of the activity of clerks and jongleurs produced only utilitarian, didactic, or unpretentiously entertaining works: homilies, hagiographic narratives, rustic songs, songs for dancing. There was still nothing to suggest either a true artistic pursuit or a vigorous creative effort. Literature could be produced only when the religious propagandists and paid performers were replaced by real poets. Of course these poets, wherever they came from, exploited the resources of the clerical culture and responded to the demands of their society. The past and the present added new richness to their songs, but they followed the impulses of their own genius and talent. Their names were Turoldus, Guillaume IX, Chrétien de Troyes. No one can say that these writers were merely mouthpieces for the aristocracy of the twelfth century. They were great artists, quite capable of individual initiative, who created the substance and form of their masterpieces. Before the Oxford *Roland* and the chansons of Guillaume IX, concludes Viscardi, there was neither French epic nor Provençal lyric. The *Roland* and these lyrics were the beginning of it all. Even if their roots reach back to a distant past, the genres to which these works belong could have come into existence only with their creation, for what they achieve is worth infinitely more than all they sum up. Thus fifty years after the publication of *Les Légendes épiques,* a critic fully versed in the most recent advances of his field could not only accept Bédier's essential assertions, but could restate them with new confidence and vigor.

However, Bédier encountered opposition even among his most faithful allies. A long and moving controversy alienated him from Ferdinand Lot, who summed it up in these terms: "Bédier told me that all literature began with one masterpiece that had no past. I argued that the masterpiece was created within a pre-established framework, and it is precisely that framework which is the subject of the debate." In other words, what interests Lot and the other "historians" is less poetic genius than the close or distant predecessors of the extant works. Although the works we know have altered the events they describe, they suggest the survival over centuries of extremely old memories. In this case, an intermediary between the ancient historic fact and the more recent *chanson de geste* would be indispensable, but it would not be the *legend* as defined by Bédier, the monastic legend that rests in the cloisters until at the right moment a monk recounts it to an inspired jongleur. In fact the oldest chansons, particularly the *Roland,* do not mention the pilgrim routes and their sanctuaries.

To speak, then, of an effective collaboration between jongleur and monk is meaningless, especially since it is rather difficult to describe exactly what such a collaboration would have involved. We must go back to the old theory of transmission from century to century — the theory of the *cantilènes* — whether we retain this deprecated term or prefer to use *ballade, complainte,* or *chant de carole.* The textual evidence that has been cited to demonstrate the existence of an oral tradition is significant: *Cantilène de Saint Faron, Fragment de la Haye, Conversio Othgerii,* the reference in *Raoul de Cambrai* to the jongleur Bertolai. This evidence is strengthened by the research on the names of Roland and Oliver and by the *Nota Emilianense.* And we cannot but admit the justice of this final remark of Lot's: "The ballad about a striking historical or anecdotal event is so spontaneous, so necessary, an occurrence among all peoples that to wish to impose its absence on our ancestors is to believe them submerged in a state of stupefaction that is not found even among the most backward of populations." Of course these ballads are lost and references to an oral tradition are rare, but this should not be surprising: according to all the evidence, there was a period when the clerks welcomed only didactic works in Latin.

Nonetheless, Lot is obliged to admit that the transition from the *complainte* to the epic proper involves a problem. He does not conceal the fact that the centuries of silence are long and uninterrupted, even when the most suspect documents are considered. He finally does admit that the poets played an important role in the elaboration of epic material.

It would be wrong, then, to say that the various objections to Bédier have been more negative than constructive. A critic outside France has given the most valuable and useful assistance to the French "historians": the eminent Spanish romance philologist, Ramón Menéndez Pidal. His long experience, his flawless scholarship, and his talent make him Bédier's most formidable adversary. It is important to mention his researches here.

Against what he justly terms Bédier's *individualist* point of view, Pidal has for more than half a century upheld a thesis he defines as *traditionalist;* by this term he means to stress both the similarities and differences between his concept and the romantic doctrines. He believes that the origins of romance literature go much farther back than the existing texts and can only be explained if a long and rich tradition of lost works is supposed — lost through the ravages of time, through the prejudice or negligence of men. Centuries of silence cannot be cited as absolute proof of the absence of literary activity. Before the appearance of the *chansons de geste*, an effective but undiscernible poetic activity was going on. In other words, the epic existed before these chansons in a *latent state*, just as lyricism, latent but full of promise, existed before Guillaume IX. It would thus be false to say, as Bédier does, that a masterpiece begins and ends with its author or, to use Lot's word, that it can be considered independently from its "cadre."

A number of notable facts come to the support of these long-pondered assertions. First there is the case of the Spanish *romancero*. Its disappearance seemed complete after a certain period; but, though invisible, it was alive. Systematic investigations were all that was needed for it to be rediscovered here and there, in America as well as in Spain. More important are what Pidal refers to as *chants romans andalous*. They are short lyric fragments in Romance Mozarabic, discovered several years ago in Hebrew or Islamic compositions written in Spain between the eleventh and thirteenth centuries. Since these works are sometimes much earlier than the chansons of Guillaume IX, it is no longer possible to claim that his poetry is the earliest example of Western lyricism. As Jeanroy had already argued, a poetry consisting essentially of *chansons de femme* preceded the courtly poetry of the troubadours; it was believed lost but its existence was not formally denied, and a happy accident brought it to life again. The silence of the centuries sometimes speaks with unexpected clarity.

When Pidal refers to a latent state, he is not content with a vague formula that would open the way to unfounded hypotheses.

The processes of creation and evolution he envisages are quite conceivable. He insists on the phenomenon of anonymity, or on what he calls successive and simultaneous collaboration, the task of revision, the unanimous and multiform interplay of the variants. That anonymity was one of the most striking characteristics of poetic production in the high Middle Ages provides evidence in itself. That the *chansons de geste* in particular have been greatly reworked is also certain. It will not be contested that those responsible for such reworkings had an altogether different attitude toward their role as writers than do men of letters today; nor will it be denied that, in adding and superimposing their own efforts, they altered to some extent the works that passed through their hands. In this respect the development of the *romancero* presents an extreme and particularly interesting example. Romances were short, episodic fragments that became popular after being detached from the *cantares de gesta*. They became part of the body of material passed on from generation to generation which every man assumed the right to retouch as he pleased, according to his own fantasy. Thanks to this proliferation of anonymous innovations, among which both the public and the performers instinctively exercised a choice, the style was modified, "depersonalized," and became more timeless, more fundamental —in a word, *traditional*. Thus an entire people actually became the author. Doubtless an individual was initially responsible for each effort that contributed to the traditionalization of a romance, but this individual did not detach himself from the group of which he was a part.

On the other hand, whoever first gave form to the romance, and whoever produced the first version of a *cantar de gesta*, assumed the highest responsibilities. Pidal urges that there be no mistake here. If the authors of such admirable works as the *Roland* and the *Cid* were great poets, they were much less interested in asserting their artistic personalities than in giving a faithful interpretation of their environment. We could thus say that, beside a people who became an author, there were authors who became a people. This double formula would apply to the entire history of the medieval epic, from its genesis to its later developments.

Pidal is not content with generalizations. He had found solid arguments in a new and penetrating analysis of the basic questions in the *Roland* debate. He first contests the *précellence* of the Oxford text, which he feels is only one version among many. Its deficiencies, such as the scene in which Ganelon is designated by Roland, vents his rage, and challenges his stepson, would be an example of the process of traditionalism. Further, Pidal has subjected the annals to a more extensive and minute examination. He emphasizes that Eginhard's version of the events at Roncevaux stands out from the rest of his chronicle because of its unusual fullness and detail, and also points out that his mention of the principal victims of the massacre is atypical. Pidal finally notes that in a first edition of the *Vita Karoli* only two names are mentioned, and Roland's is added later. He concludes that the initial silence of the official chroniclers was broken because the public at large, influenced by the popular narratives, both preserved the memory of the event and attributed to Roland an increasingly important and tragic role in the battle. Thus Eginhard would have spoken in such detail only because, after the beginning of the ninth century, it was impossible to ignore the development of a veritable oral epic at the boundaries of clerical historiography.

Other arguments confirm this point of view. Certain Carolingian annals, which are fully substantiated by Islamic chroniclers, admit that the Saracens played an important role during the 778 expedition, not only by inciting Charlemagne to undertake it but also by participating in the battles that led to the final defeat. Some of these same annals speak of an immense tribute of gold offered to the French by the infidels, to ensure their departure. Finally, one of them describes a miracle in which the sun was slowed in its course to aid Charlemagne. During the tenth century the oral epic, which had rivaled history ever since the ninth century, enriched the chronicles with new details, some real and some legendary.

Reservations can certainly be offered in opposition to these conclusions, particularly with regard to the deficiencies of the Oxford version and the emendations in the chronicles, but there is no doubt of the strength of the traditionalist explanation. Bédier sees the work in terms of its structure and dates its origin from the moment that this structure took definite form and significance in the artist's mind. Pidal and Lot are concerned with the framework, the various elements that led to the composition of the work, no matter how original, by providing the author with material, themes, means of expression, and outlines that were already very exciting. Pidal also stresses the transformations that many medieval works underwent even at their birth. In other words, he establishes an evolution or sequence that separates the poem from the successive contributions to its construction, amelioration, or alteration. Thus the unique and conclusive creation that Bédier proposed is, in Pidal's estimation, subordinate to a sum of convergent efforts, of which even the most lowly might have been forcefully effective. The variance between these two arguments is the result of two different attitudes toward the phenomenon of poetic creation — one is resolutely individualistic, the other sociologically inspired. Since poetic creation is both an individual act and a social phenomenon, it is hardly surprising that solid factual support can be found for either point of view. But we cannot help wondering whether, in this heated debate over origins, all disagreements might finally be the result of a simple misunderstanding. It is logical to attempt a reconciliation.

For example, we might subscribe to Italo Siciliano's suggestions in his *Origines des chansons de geste*. After distinguishing between legend and poem, he makes this statement: Bédier admitted the literary genre of the *chanson de geste* was not a *proles sine matre creata*, and Lot had to confess that we know nothing positive about this 'mother' before the eleventh century. The former is bound to the reality of the text; the latter believes in the necessity of a theory. Now literary history allows both." As against Bédier, Siciliano then posits the existence of an enduring impulse that arouses and maintains interest in certain illustrious figures over the centuries, creating a *legend* around them. But this legend "is not the poem. One day the legend, transformed into a poetic theme, becomes the property of a particular person; it submits to the influence of a specific period, takes on either the modest cloak given it by the jongleur or the eternal form created by genius, and dies to be reborn as a *poem*. From this moment on, but only then, the poet is all and the masterpiece, when it exists, is at once the end and the beginning, as Bédier would have it."

This amounts to saying that we must support both Bédier's adversaries and Bédier himself: the former as regards the legends and the poetic language utilized by the authors of the *chansons de geste;* the latter in the particular study of each of these chansons, insofar as it is a poem or, if one prefers, an original literary work. Doubtless this treatment is too schematic, too simplified, since the individual and the collective, albeit in variable proportions, coincide in the preparatory phase as well as in the active phase of poetic creation. The poet uses a pre-existing language, as does anyone who speaks. This language imposes on him a whole range of concepts, themes, and verbal mechanisms which, in their highest forms, govern his thought and sensibility. Of course it is a personal act when he takes advantage of his resources and demonstrates the capacities of his talent. But his creation is also valuable because of the various anonymous and collective efforts by which it has profited, and because of the poetry already contained in the means of expression or the materials he, often after others, has exploited. The complexity of the situation forbids absolute categorization. It is not with rigid methodology but with an intelligence sensitive to the finest nuances that one can hope to comprehend it.

In conclusion we should attempt to particularize views by applying them to the *Roland*. As a point of departure, we might take the superiority of the Oxford text, on which not even Pidal has succeeded in casting doubt. Despite its faults, the manuscript is the best and oldest in our possession. The version of which it is a copy, and most probably a faithful one, is also the best and oldest we can hope to approach at the present. Every attempt to dissect the compact whole that constitutes the *Roland*, in order to find a more primitive version behind it, is doomed to failure. Nothing prevents us from thinking of this poem as a unique work of art, written around 1100 by a poet of genius whose name was perhaps Turoldus. But obviously this does not necessarily mean that, before this work of art, no epic breath had stirred the themes and characters it immortalizes.

The author of the *Roland* might well have had legendary tales at his disposal. But since his genius shows us that we can expect an astonishing creativity, and since the accessible evidence is very slight, it does not follow that we must specifically relegate these legends, as does Bédier, to the custody of monks in eleventh-century sanctuaries. We do not have to minimize their epic significance or associate them with some pseudo-historical or didactic Latin text. This would be to limit the range of possibilities excessively: such a precise understanding of the Roncevaux legends would be impossible. We know neither their age nor their origins; we are ignorant of the circumstances in which they were born and propagated. The texts are just as deceptive when they mention the legends as when they are silent. We do not know when the character of Roland became legendary to the exclusion of Eggihard and Anselm, or whether it was in popular or clerical circles that this came about; we do not know the form by which he was made famous, whether it was oral narrative, *complainte*, or *cantilène*. It is equally impossible to be certain that truly epic qualities existed in these narratives and songs. Every element must be taken into consideration; to exclude any one would be to make a perfectly arbitrary choice.

As we approach the year 1100, evidence can be gathered. The documents that connect the names of Roland and Oliver suggest that in the eleventh century the theme of the two young warriors' companionship already existed and enjoyed wide familiarity. A text, probably in a Romance language, and already appealing to the imagination, was doubtless responsible for this success, but it is unlikely that this text was a *chanson de Roland* since the onomastic custom that appears at the beginning of the eleventh century gives priority to Oliver. Aebischer was forced to postulate a primitive *Girard de Viane* by which this priority, inconceivable after a *Roland*, would be better explained. From both the *Fragment de la Haye* and the *Nota Emilianense* we are led to envisage, not the existence of a single poem nearly one hundred years before the date assigned to the Oxford *Roland*, but rather that of a fairly extensive epic activity, even a vast oral epic literature of a "fluid" nature, which had not yet made distinctions between the various cycles; it was not channeled, and the currents could as easily come together as diverge. In this perspective, the development of the technique that is so successfully put to use in the Oxford text no longer raises a problem. With the basis of unequaled artistic skill, it presupposes a whole series of progressive adjustments, beginning no doubt with the liturgical readings and culminating in the irregular *laisses* that were so perfectly adapted to the dramatic and mimed declamation of the *chansons de geste*.

A conclusion can now be drawn: the eleventh century was marked by many distinct efforts, noteworthy and insignificant, poetically effective and not, from which the author of the Oxford *Roland* could have profited greatly. For lack of evidence we must be careful not to date this *latent* epic activity too far back in the past. More exactly, we must accept the practical impossibility of establishing a direct connection, or even a series of precise stages, between the event of 778 and the Roland epic. A bond was doubtless maintained, but to propose dates, locations, and forms, or to define the steps, would be presumptuous. By their very nature the legends elude our grasp. Since we have been somewhat enlightened about the eleventh century, must we persist in straining the impenetrable silence that separates it from the eighth? This silence has spoken before, and it may again, but we have to assume that whatever it conceals will never appear in a completely clear manner, and will give rise to new discussions.

The latent activity that traditionalism would have us visualize involves an obscure development over a period of centuries. It is still possible to maintain that, at the end of this activity, individuals could have acted decisively — real authors of originality and creativity. The reversal from Oliver-Roland to Roland-Oliver proves that mutations could suddenly occur, and that in this case the author of the mutation could well have been responsible for the Oxford version. Despite the extensive collective and anonymous effort behind them, we must ask whether the extant chansons — particularly the Bodleian *Roland* — are not authentic literary works, produced by men of uneven gifts but frequent talent. These men, who were both modest and ambitious, could have gone beyond introducing occasional interpolations into the gestes while being involved in a kind of successive collaboration. It is quite possible that some of them produced complete revisions, after re-evaluating what subjects were most likely to be stimulating to the emotions and imagination.

Let us look, by way of comparison, at the different treatments that Béroul and Thomas have so effectively given to the Tristan legend. By adding the idea of *mutation* to the term *tradition*, I hope to have suggested that the high position granted to the Poet by the individualists should be retained, despite the concessions that must henceforth be made to the traditionalists. The Oxford *Roland*, even as it is the product of a collective development, would also be the result of a true artistic re-creation realized at the end of the eleventh century. Why not? There is no reason to deny that it is Turoldus' masterpiece — if the last line is a signature — just as *Le Cid* is Corneille's masterpiece. I fell particularly sure about this statement because the comparison with *Le Cid* was made by Pidal himself, and because it should also satisfy the most loyal of Bédier's followers! I would not dare to suggest that we are on the eve of a reconciliation, however. There are still too many violent antagonisms, too many occasions and pretexts for mutual accusation.

Thus, however little we are inspired by individualism or traditionalism, however little we share Bédier's rigorous regard for the texts or Pidal's consideration of the most humble and impersonal attempts, we cannot but see that each line of the Oxford *Roland* is the offering of an exceptional artist, and part of an integral whole that is its own beginning and end. But we can also hear the echo of all the voices that the author united, all the spirits that helped his own to be moved, the voices and spirits that together represent the heroic France of the Crusades and of feudal chivalry, the literate France of the clerks and — why not? — of the jongleurs; he was heir to a long cultural tradition and creator of new forms of expression.

Certainly we should like to be more specific and definite. But to have formulated a unified and logical opinion based on solid ideas about the genesis of a work like the *Roland* is something. Perhaps we have also surmounted the vexing contradictions of a seemingly insoluble debate. In any case, it is a great satisfaction to be able to rely on the Oxford text and to read it with the reasonable belief that, whatever its antecedents might have been, it is probably the creation of a true poet.

SIX · COMPOSITION,
UNITY, AND MEANING

The *Chanson de Roland* may be conveniently divided into four parts: the betrayal, the battle, the punishment of the pagans, and the punishment of Ganelon. The narrative surrounds, situates, and explains the battle; its conclusion reveals the meaning and consequences of this central episode. A single idea dominates the poem: Roland and Charlemagne are presented as incarnations of the pride, heroism, and faith of an entire nation, and are invested with a sacred mission, the Crusade. What could be more simple — if not banal — than this outline and scheme? It might seem that we are confronted with a subject for melodrama. Yet Bédier was right when he said, "Turold's work is admirable despite, rather than because of, its subject." The wealth of the *Roland* is not superficial. It will only be discovered by the reader who makes the effort to find it and places his trust in the poet.

By assuming at the outset that Spain has been almost completely conquered by Charlemagne, the author of the *Roland* is mocking history but obeying a logical necessity. If the old emperor is to play the role we know, he has to find success beyond the Pyrenees. But then the disaster at Roncevaux is not easily explained. Since Charles is victorious, it seems unlikely that his rear guard should fall into an ambush and perish while he is recrossing the mountains. There is only one way to resolve this contradiction: a formidable adversary, the king of Saragossa, has been spared. This presents new problems. If he has been spared, it is because he seems to have spontaneously surrendered and provided the needed guarantees. He was at bay, with no hope of victory. Why he immediately breaks the peace he has just sought, without regard for the hostages he has surrendered, is unclear. It only takes a little treachery to break a sworn oath, and it is easy to attribute a great deal of it to the pagan Marsile. Still his treachery cannot have the appearance of a mere suicide: he must have been encouraged by a sudden promising chance to deal Charlemagne and the French a mortal blow, at little expense to himself.

Who better than a traitor could provide this opportunity? Perhaps this seems a facile and predictable solution. And it would be, if the traitor were an ordinary one, but this is exactly what our poet did not want. Instinctively sensing the difficulties, he sets Ganelon and Roland face to face at the emperor's council, in the great argument provoked by Blancandrin's offer. He implies strong resentments between the men that erupt over the basic problem of peace and war. The debate concludes when Roland chooses Ganelon to bear the message to the Saracens, and this choice provides at once the motive, the opportunity, and the means for committing the crime. It would be difficult to handle this subject, which Bédier terms melodramatic, with greater elegance and mastery.

If we are to appreciate the merits of our poet, we must go beyond a consideration of unity and watch him put each detail in place within his creation. As soon as Blancandrin reveals his plan of feigned surrender to Marsile, the author suggests that the French, surfeited with victory, are tired and eager to return home. "Offer riches to Charles . . . he can then pay his mercenaries handsomely; tell him that he has warred long enough in this land, that he should return to France, to Aix." The part that this incentive is to play will soon be apparent when the French are faced with the decision between war and peace. Before this, the author brings it in again at an opportune moment, when Blancandrin says to Charlemagne: "You have stayed long enough in this country; you should return to France, to Aix." By repetition, the author stresses the factor that will govern the situation and determine later developments — the way has been very delicately prepared.

These foreshadowings define the atmosphere and help to explain the underlying causes of the drama; they also add life and new dimensions to the characters. Blancandrin is no ordinary messenger. He realizes that certain tendencies in the French mentality will serve his treacherous plan. From the very outset, he has known what can divide his enemies and undermine their conquerors' morale. It does not take him long to read Ganelon's soul, and he profits beyond all expectation from the situation his peace offering has helped to create. In short, Blancandrin not only inspires the message he bears, he exploits it and expands its effect. Thus he ceases to be a contrivance and becomes one of the principal figures in the drama. We can no longer doubt that if a *Chanson de Roland* existed without Blancandrin, it was different from the *Chanson de Roland* we know, constructed on another basis. It is true that as soon as the treacherous pact is concluded, he disappears. But surely an author has the right to forget someone who has become expendable.

Let us proceed to the great decisive scene, the council of the French. The debate is closely connected to the introduction, the Saracen council, in that it echoes from beginning to end the theme of French weariness suggested in those first verses. Roland realizes what is tempting to many of his companions in Blancandrin's offer. The intensity of his intervention is proof enough. By invoking the fate of Basan and Basile, he hopes to give the French new strength while casting blame on the fainthearted councilors, whom he feels are responsible for the death of the two messengers. Ganelon, with good reason, thinks that Roland is referring to him and this explains the violence of his retort. It is certainly not the first time he and his stepson have clashed over the question of whether an exhausting and deadly war should be prolonged, or ended by the first advantageous settlement. Both the war and the enemy are extraordinary. The sequel reveals the value of Marsile's word and, more important, shows that Marsile, finally supported by all Islam, is the incarnation of a cause with which the Christians cannot compromise in practice or in principle. Because of his pride and rashness, Roland may seem to love war for its own sake. In reality he is the only one who understands that one does not compromise when fighting for God. Thus Roland disputes Ganelon's questionable advice. He also defies the wisdom of the faithful Naimes and even the sympathetic Oliver. The apotheosis that rewards his sacrifice is more elevated than that of his most heroic companions and illustrates the merit of his decision. It is shown also by the obligations his death imposes on Charlemagne the day after the battle, and through the punishment his stepfather incurs. The poet thus unfolds the drama in a scene that is wholly at one with all that has gone before and all that follows.

When he is appointed by Roland, Ganelon is enraged, and the conditions under which he expresses this rage are extraordinary. The meaning of Roland's earlier speech is clear. His stepfather is irritated by the intransigence with which he is so familiar; it shocks his rationality as much as it offends his deeper emotions. He violently pleads the cause of peace. Naimes approves, with the serenity of a spirit free of afterthoughts, and easily gains unanimous support. Charles, who was doubtful at the outset, now replies with a simple question that implies acquiescence if not approbation: "And now, who shall we send to Marsile?" Naimes, Roland, Oliver, and Turpin successively offer to carry out the mission, which they clearly see as dangerous. The emperor brushes them aside with an indignant gesture: "Woe to him who names one of the twelve peers!" Roland chooses this moment, in the midst of the oppressive uneasiness, to say: "Let it be Ganelon, my stepfather!" — "An excellent choice," reply the French. Ganelon does not see it that way: "Fool, what is this madness? I am your stepfather, everyone knows that. If God wills that I return from Marsile's camp, I will do you such harm as will last the rest of your days!" What a strange emotion, and how sudden! This anxiety is hardly consistent with the proud, ennobling gesture with which he has just thrown down his sable cloak, and is unworthy of the baron that all acknowledge him to be. His selection is a mark of their esteem, and yet he is indignant. The projected mission is peaceful and thus without apparent danger. He advised it, and yet he is afraid. Furthermore, Charlemagne has not yet spoken and nothing is decided.

The problems facing the critic here can well be imagined. We might challenge the arrangement of the scene as it appears in the Oxford manuscript, or accuse the poet of clumsiness and inconsistency. But first let us try to live out the situation and put ourselves in the character's place. Though approved by the French council, Ganelon has not forgotten his recent altercation with Roland. Like his stepson, he has invested his proposals with a passion that has not subsided, despite his success. For he thinks he can read Roland's thoughts. He dreads an energetic counterattack by this proud, rigid man. When appointed by him, Ganelon immediately suspects the most foul designs. He assumes that Roland, with Basan and Basile in mind, believes in the perfidy of the pagans and at heart hopes this belief is right. It seems to Ganelon that Roland is indifferent to his own stepfather's fate. Perhaps he even enjoys seeing Ganelon exposed to these great dangers. Along with his twelve peers, Roland is still the one to benefit from the emperor's solicitude. What does this favoritism mean? With everyone against him, it seems a conspiracy. Ganelon's immediate reaction is understandable, for such an appointment amounts to an insult. The worst of it is that it is established without question: Charlemagne is only too happy to confirm it. The victim cannot think for a moment of escape. Fear is probably mingled with indignation in Ganelon's hasty reply, and Roland remarks on it with a scornful smile. That is all his enraged stepfather needs to hurl the fateful challenge: he will carry out his mission and, if he survives, revenge himself.

Why does he question his survival when he has just affirmed Marsile's good faith? The truth is that Ganelon's weakness is a consuming desire for peace. He has lost the spirit of sacrifice and has succumbed to the allure of earthbound pleasures. Blinded by the hope aroused by Blancandrin's offer, he discounted the fate of Basan and Basile. Now that an identical fate threatens him, he loses his fine assurance. He longs for peace — not to negotiate it, at great risk to himself, but to enjoy it. He would probably have been more prudent had it occurred to him at the outset that he would be taken at his word and charged with delivering the message that answers his wishes. When Roland forces him to confront reality, his rage and confusion are understandable. Vulnerable as he is to hatred and emotion, he can hardly keep control of his words or gestures. He can only reveal the troubled depths of a soul in which a long-standing hatred is mingled with nostalgia for peace and homeland, with wounded pride, the panic of fear, and the thirst for revenge.

Nothing should be changed in the Oxford text: what might have raised a question of authenticity instead establishes the marvelous vision of the poet. He skillfully unites the elements in this concrete situation and develops their consequences through the most complex psychological mechanisms. The atmosphere in which he locates his characters has been carefully and subtly prepared, and within the spirits of these well-placed characters lie the causes of the drama he has invented. The sure and inexorable course of the action accords with the logic of their natures. The poet is too clever to oversimplify this fatal evolution, and he probably enjoys the complexity because it allows him to display his skill. The council scene is decisive in paving the way for all that follows — but it does not determine the destiny of the protagonists. If the battle of Roncevaux is to occur, Ganelon must allow his desire for revenge to push him to the extreme of treason. And Roland must help his mortal enemy to attain his ends. We shall now look at how this is achieved, and evaluate each element in the process.

Ganelon is certainly not a man to utter vain threats. But the French are not in a position to suspect that the respectable baron will use the mission to effect his revenge. They let him go, not without anxiety, and despite the ill omen that marked the symbolic delivery of the glove at the close of the conference. His men crowd around him sympathetically. They evoke his prowess, his favorable reputation, and above all the high lineage that puts him on a level with the twelve peers and ought to win him the same privileges. Nothing could better serve to nourish his rancor.

It is Blancandrin, however, who makes the first advances during the journey. It is hardly surprising that Marsile's clever messenger should return to his favorite theme, a leitmotiv since the first lines of the poem. That Ganelon should respond to such an appeal is even less surprising. To speak of a war that continues endlessly and irrationally is necessarily to speak of Roland. The two men, soon accomplices, have no trouble reaching an agreement: as the sole obstacle to the universally desired peace, Charlemagne's nephew must perish. Neither of the speakers thinks to recall the true character of the struggle that opposes two religions. This lack of principle blinds Ganelon to the real scope of the pact he has just concluded: henceforth it is not vengeance, but treason. Actually he has still to propose a plan when he appears before Marsile. It almost seems that he will regain his self-control at the last minute. The tone he adopts and the unexpected and extraordinary speech he delivers have puzzled even Bédier. Ganelon's provocative insolence is certainly calculated, for the poet takes care to bring it to our attention. But the plan that inspires it is not clear.

When he speaks thus, Ganelon knows he is risking his life. He has barely overcome his fear of death, but now seems eager to share the fate of Basan and Basile. Revenge is more precious to him than safety, and yet he jeopardizes his opportunity to enact it, as well as his own life. It may be that he counts on Blancandrin's opportune intervention to save him from the pagans' wrath. This does not explain why he unleashes their anger in the first place. He risks everything: Why? The pagans are discouraged and prepared for complete submission. As Bédier supposes, Ganelon undoubtedly hopes to revive their combative spirit. He will need all their courage and hatred if, as he plans, Roland is to be defeated in the ambush. Bédier further suggests that Ganelon also wants to create a grievance other than his own fear. For him to feel that Roland has placed him within a hair's breadth of death would better justify his revenge and his treason.

But Ganelon seems rather to be struggling with certain unavowed fears. He has revealed his anxiety to the French. He has now to prove to himself that he is not a coward, that, if he wishes, he can match the audacity of his unruly stepson when confronting this great danger. Thus he acts as Roland might in his place. He is convinced that he has been gratuitously slighted and scorned. Ganelon believes that he is free to dare anything, that legally and morally he will be justified. Still he is careful to establish a distinction between Charlemagne and Roland. Though he now feels he has the right to harm Roland by any means, his obligations to the emperor hold good. Ganelon praises Charlemagne in stirring terms. He persuades himself that the deed of which he dreams, in assuring a lasting peace, serves the real interests of the French and their supreme leader. So Ganelon incurs risks that not long since his "overdelicate heart" would have kept him from. In apparent contradiction to what he thinks or pretends to think about peace and Marsile's good faith, he does his best to revive the treachery and belligerence of the king. Marsile is called upon to become his accomplice.

If the astonishing and dangerous part that Ganelon plays can be thus explained, other difficulties of the text remain unsolved. Ganelon's verbal instructions are of a conciliatory nature. He is also the bearer of a letter, supposedly intended to substantiate his words. But this letter contains innuendoes and demands that will scarcely facilitate a peaceful settlement. Perhaps Charlemagne changed his mind at the last minute and wants the guarantees that the council had thought unnecessary. If so, he has risked putting his messenger in an impossible situation, justifying treachery in advance. In fact, the pagans are indignant over the contents of the letter. But they realize that the letter is unrelated to Ganelon's speech. Their anger is directed against the unfaithful messenger — "Ganelon is mad. Anyone who has spoken as he has no longer deserves to live."

At this point, Blancandrin intervenes. He could certainly have spoken sooner. But after what went on during their trip he could hardly have foreseen the attitude Ganelon was going to adopt. He overcomes his surprise with difficulty and is therefore slow to react. The threat hanging over Ganelon finally decides him: Saragossa's last hope must not disappear with this man, whatever he might be willing to risk. The tumult immediately subsides, promises are exchanged, and the plan is drawn up. Ganelon dares to swear on the cross of his sword. Now at the depths of ignominy, he receives payment for his treachery. This is what hatred and misunderstanding have made of a reputable baron; henceforth neither his legitimate weaknesses nor the injustice of which he was the victim can earn him the slightest excuse. His very virtues, which passion enlists in its service, enhance the odiousness of his crime. The poet knew how this should be expressed, and it is useless to try to trap him in a fault.

Ganelon has committed his betrayal. But only the first act of the treason has been accomplished. Marsile will be at Roncevaux; it is up to Ganelon to lure his stepson there as well. He knows that when Charlemagne's army leaves a hostile country it covers itself with a choice rear guard, under Roland's command. But if the usual precautions are not taken, his plan will fail.

He must make sure that the agreement and securities obtained at Saragossa do not allay every fear. The part that still has to be worked out is obviously both delicate and perilous, and should not be underestimated. Ganelon will choose Roland for the rear guard exactly as Roland chose him for the peace mission: in the middle of the council, during a debate, and in response to a question from the emperor. The parallel is certainly predictable. However, Ganelon risks exposing himself, and saving his victim, when he mentions Roland's name with an impatience that cannot but strike the audience. Everyone remembers the challenge he has issued. His interest in the rear guard and its leader arouses suspicion: he has just come to terms with the enemy, but is concerned for the general safety of the French. Why does Charlemagne hesitate to put the suspect under precautionary guard and to assure the safety of Roland and his company?

At this point, Ganelon's extreme cleverness becomes apparent. He realizes that he must appoint Roland himself since it is essential that the French fear for Roland, and thus for his men as well. Then the choice that is crucial to the success of his plot will be forced on Charlemagne, and his nephew will feel compelled to claim it for himself as a glorious privilege. Ganelon has certainly said too much to be able to deny his crime later. But he is more concerned with revenge than with his own life. He has already shown this by braving Marsile's rage. His courage deserves a better cause, but it can only enhance the success of his sinister plot — until it finally exposes him to the worst of punishments. Confronted with the suspicions that his attitude has created, he conceals this courage. The French know the man and his weaknesses. They saw his anxiety as he left for Saragossa, but not his bold defiance of the pagans. If guilty, Ganelon would flee or keep silent; at least they think so. A doubt, by which the villain profits, lingers in their minds.

Here Roland himself becomes his enemy's accomplice. He refuses the reinforcements offered him. And Charlemagne does not dare impose them on him, for to accept such aid would be to reveal fear or to disbelieve in heroism. To take precautions, unquestionably prudent but perhaps unnecessary would be to lose face. As for Charles, he loves his nephew too much to risk wounding his pride or compromising his glory. Anguish is Charlemagne's lot; his very nobility condemns him to silence and prevents him from acting. Ganelon has foreseen this, and it becomes part of his plan. No one will miss the rendezvous at Roncevaux, and no one will be there who is not compelled by the diabolical lucidity of the traitor or by the splendid folly of the victim. As Bédier has said, Roncevaux is inevitable. But fate acts in accord with the nature of the characters and becomes an expression of their free will.

It cannot be too often stressed that the drama of Roncevaux is at heart a human drama, initiated by Roland's pride. This pride creates, sustains, and effects the expression of Ganelon's hatred, which is at once blind and clever. It exploits for its own satisfaction the same excesses of pride it seeks to destroy. It is both logical and paradoxical; the better to harm and triumph, it imitates the ungovernable pride that it finds unbearable. Thus Ganelon, the respected and wise man who prefers negotiation to battle and peace to war, renounces all he had defended in order to confront all he fears. And Roland, transported by prodigious bravery and superhuman heroism, faithful to himself to the bitter end, rushes toward the death which is being readied for him and which he is helping to prepare.

Up to this point, God has not intervened or at least has restricted himself to obscure warnings. Ganelon, who risks all for a moment of evil joy, is no longer concerned with the Crusade lest he see the abyss of damnation before him. Roland loves war for its own sake. He enjoys the rude pleasures of combat and he dreams of conquest. The sentiment of honor dictates all he says, inspires all his deeds. His passions are noble, but earthly as well, and we still do not know whether they should be condemned or forgiven, admired or criticized. At Roncevaux Roland's destiny will be decided, and God will speak. For at Roncevaux the drama, like all that is human, must change direction and find its culmination beyond the limited horizons of this world. A new task awaits our poet. Deep emotional understanding and infallible architectural skill no longer suffice. He must maintain the qualities with which he has constructed the poem's splendid introduction, uniting intuition and reason in a subtle play of parallels and contrasts, perspectives and striking transitions. He must transcend the human reality, pass from drama to epic, from epic to myth. But we already know that we can expect a great deal from his genius.

The symmetrical scenes, which contrast Marsile's twelve knights in the front rank of his army with the twelve peers led by Roland, stand out in an examination of the preliminaries to the battle. They recall the two contrasting scenes that begin the poem and lead us from the court of Saragossa to the camp of Charlemagne. In the French camp, serenity is united with loyalty; at Saragossa, anxiety is bound to treachery. True to his simple and effective methods, the author is careful to build the tension before pitting Roland's little band against Marsile's rough horde. He is more concerned with the action of their minds in explaining the events, and so he suspends the course of the drama rather than pushing it forward.

In fact, nothing has been decided when the enemy suddenly appears, and Roland and Oliver begin their moving debate. Roland is still free to change his destiny. He has only to sound the oliphant, and Roncevaux will not be Roncevaux. But Roland would no longer be the Roland whom Ganelon hates and knows too well to be denied his revenge, the Roland whom Oliver loves and despairs of ever winning over to his own wisdom. The debate between Roland and Oliver is built on a conventional comparison, renewed through vivid character portrayal. The theme is not only rich in humanity and forceful poetry, but also plays an essential part in the poem as a principal structural element. Oliver's brief comment during the argument over the peace mission prepares the way, and the debate itself marks the end of a progression that culminates in Roland's folly. To invoke Basan and Basile and to reject the idea of negotiation with Marsile is not enough. Roland must provoke Ganelon's rage, and thus his treason. By insisting on a dangerous post and refusing reinforcements, he implements his enemy's plan. At the last moment, abandoning all caution, surer than ever of his prowess — perhaps unmindful of the fate of his men and of the greater interests of Christianity — he blindly rushes into a battle that from the start is doomed by his own fault.

At the end of the argument between the two friends, Turpin points out that Christian duty is as important as fealty and honor. Although Roland knows this, he is afraid that his reputation will become the subject of scornful songs. Yet God reserves the highest favors for him. In a new debate, parallel to the first but with the roles reversed, Roland will earn this favor, assisted by his very rashness. Surely this is a construct of the highest order.

As for the battle itself, the poet is clearly more interested in significance than in events. We have just seen his careful definition of the moral climate in which the battle occurs. He wants the eventual outcome to be clear. Thus, in a famous strophe the fatal omens accumulate, contrasting with the French cries of

"Montjoie." The tragic and mournful lines, repeated like a knell, echo the very sorrow of nature. The poet scorns surprise effects or theatrical gestures. He wants us to look back and ahead with him. He is less interested in our curiosity than in an essential participation in the emotion and meaning he conveys. But, for all this, his descriptions do not suffer.

The picture of the battle in the Oxford *Roland* is ordered, precise, full of brilliance and movement. Basically it consists of two parts. In the first encounter, the French triumph easily over their opponents, and Turpin can cry: "The first blow is ours!" In the second conflict, which balances but contrasts with the first, the Christians fall one after another despite the redoubled efforts of Oliver, Turpin, and Roland. Such parallels and contrasts are familiar by now, and their dual purpose is again apparent. They not only give aesthetic equilibrium to the narrative, but also clarify and emphasize its meaning. This is why the battle prolongs the debate between Roland and Oliver, which itself sums up the entire drama and makes it more painful. The poet has presented the two heroes with equal sympathy and does not choose between them. The changing events make one right, then the other, justifying both Roland's confidence and Oliver's fear. Beyond the noise of battle, the clanking of arms, and the cries of soldiers, there resounds the echo of an inner conflict that rends the conscience. These related conflicts will find a single conclusion as the true meaning of the poem emerges.

Roland sincerely thinks he will win and, when he sees Marsile's squadrons approach, generously doubts that he has been betrayed. His confidence and his illusions are buoyed for a time by the intoxication of battle. Little by little, as he sees his men fall, he understands his error and his position changes. Again defying the wise Oliver's advice, he grasps his horn and sounds a long note. Since it is too late to be of any use, his decision to sound the horn is puzzling. Defeat is certain; none of the French can escape death. Charles's nephew must regret the loss of the battle, but he cannot regret having undertaken it. He no longer has that right. His companions have perished without reproach or complaint. As Bédier says, "Roland owes them this ending; they have earned it. He owes it to their lord Charles and his premonitions; he owes it to Ganelon, whose plot was a tribute." Roland does not need to condemn his decision, for he is justified not only by his own heroism but also by that of his men. But he sounds the horn because this justification is no longer enough for him.

Roland sees with growing sorrow the extent of the sacrifices he has exacted from the others and himself. He does not have to repudiate his heroism, but from this moment it is more a source of pain than pride to him. He gradually sheds his arrogance. He knows that he has overreacted to a traitor's challenge and to his own impulse to stifle gossip. He realizes that everything at Roncevaux is for the triumph and glory of an infinitely sacred cause. Henceforth he wants only to think of this cause. Affection, gratitude, and esteem impel him to assure his comrades an honorable grave, but a sacred duty also demands that he do his utmost to limit a disaster that threatens to destroy Christianity completely. So he finally summons Charlemagne. He promises to the dead the homage that is their due and recognizes the real meaning of their sacrifice. Roland recalls that the true framework of the battle of Roncevaux is the Crusade. Above all, forgetting himself, he consents to an act of true humility. Saints and martyrs know that in the service of God, whatever one dares or aspires to, one can never do enough. But they also know that their valor has no value except as an offering, a gift to the Creator.

If this is not what the poet meant, then the silence, followed by the notes of the horn, would be pointless. But they clearly represent the sharp contrast between Roland's spiritual states during the crucial moments of the battle. Let us examine the parallel movement of the narrative after Roland first sounds the horn.

Repudiated by Oliver and certain of defeat, Charles' nephew is in despair. His temples are burst from the mortal effort of sounding the horn. Still other trials await him. Again thrown into the conflict, he sees the survivors about him falling, one after another. Among them are those dearest to his heart, Oliver and Turpin. His own pain is such that he knows his time is running out. An abyss as deep as his pride was great seems to open before him, and everything in and around him begins to change. Charlemagne hears and understands his final message. Roland has the precious and profound consolation, after their dispute, of being reconciled with Oliver, who is on the verge of death. Against all hope, he sees victory smiling at him. Charlemagne's bugles and the cries of "Montjoie," now so close, echo the last weak notes of the oliphant. Marsile, his hand severed by Durendal, has fled, followed by his last routed squadrons. Roland is still master of the battlefield.

But this small triumph is not enough. Other privileges are reserved for him. With great difficulty Roland has brought the lifeless French together, and he sees Turpin give them a final and consoling benediction. Though he could not save their lives, he has at least the satisfaction of ministering to their souls. His own death will be the holiest and most beautiful of all. In the evening of a victorious battle, his body free of any wound save that inflicted by his own sorrow, he is the last to die. But first he is able to bid farewell to his sword Durendal, to Charlemagne, and to his beloved France. With his face turned toward a conquered Spain, he utters a calm and serene prayer. Finally, beating his breast and holding his glove up to God as a symbol of fealty, he sees a procession of angels coming toward him, sent by God to welcome his heroic and martyred soul. To echo Bédier's phrases, each scene of mourning in the battle's epilogue is also a scene of glory. "The Passion of Roland is both absolute pain and absolute joy."

We know that the poet's use of symmetry and contrast is supremely masterful. We are familiar with his ability to combine intimations of the future with echoes of what has happened and to construct the most skillful progressions. His is a technique adapted to the demands of poetry and aided by an acute sense of human reality. But like a cathedral's architect, he also knows how to elevate our gaze, up through vigorous ascending lines and arcs, to the horizon of the spiritual world. The splendid movement in the *Chanson* which begins with the sounding of the horn and proceeds to Roland's beatification proves at least that the ambitions of the work are high. There is some question about whether these aspirations are realized and whether the level of excellence, once reached, is sustained. Some critics raise such points because they are disappointed in the Baligant episode.

Roland is dead, but he is both victorious and vindicated. God has welcomed him in heaven with the honors reserved for saints. A more glorious conclusion would be difficult to imagine. The noble victims of the battle must be buried; Saragossa, now defenseless, must be occupied and the traitor, who is already in chains, must be executed. A few verses would suffice to describe these three scenes and give the poem its obvious epilogue. But the poet is not satisfied with this solution, and to criticize him for it would be unfair. Of course everything that occurs at Roncevaux is the fault of either Roland or Ganelon. But their mistake, especially Ganelon's, is to try to resolve a private quarrel through the battle. They are all the more guilty in that their dispute breaks out over the course of the Crusade itself; and they neglect to discuss that greater cause, one out of hatred, the other through pride. Ganelon believes that he is taking revenge against one man, while in fact he is betraying a sacred cause. Roland, in his eagerness to answer his stepfather's challenge, exposes Christendom to a catastrophe. Ganelon maintains his criminal error to the end, however, and Roland regains his perspective; it is too late to save his life or the lives of his men, but not to die a crusader, a true soldier of Christ. His death affirms the principles and virtues, the mission and obligations, that surround a universal and eternal cause.

There is something too holy and absolute in Roland's nobility to allow a light revenge. After Roland's martydom, God must speak as clearly on earth as he has in heaven. In his name, Christianity must offer proof of its power to all Islam. Charles' revenge must equal his pain at the loss he has just sustained. Only one adversary is worthy of him; the emir Baligant. Whoever sees that Roland's death is the very opposite of a local, episodic occurrence will understand the richness of the twofold epilogue with which the *Chanson* concludes.

Roland has just died when Charlemagne arrives at Roncevaux; in the distance is a cloud of dust raised by Marsile's army in its desperate flight. Leaving a guard with the dead, the emperor takes up the chase. At his request, God performs a miracle; he stops the sun in its course and the French drive the enemy into the waters of the Ebro. Still armed, Charles encamps on the spot, and a mysterious and prophetic vision disturbs his sleep. At Saragossa, while Marsile weeps and the others curse their idols, the queen Bramidoine mentions Baligant's name for the first time. Seven years ago they had sought his aid — will he come? He does land, finally, and quickly advances, followed by multitudes from the East. In a few hours he joins Marsile and receives his homage. Baligant's messengers challenge Charlemagne and his name at Roncevaux as the French are embalming the bodies of Roland, Turpin, and Oliver.

There are several possible objections to this sequence. The emir's arrival is very sudden. It seems unlikely that he would have sent no word for seven years. If he had announced his arrival even a few hours in advance, Marsile would have waited. Faced with united forces of Spain and the East, the French would have been defeated. One could search for signs of interpolation here. But, despite such arguments, this episode is organically linked with the rest of the poem. First, Charlemagne's vision indirectly predicts it. Second, the episode postpones Marsile's punishment and the capture of Saragossa, each an expected sequel to the battle of Roncevaux. Above all, it fulfills the need for a higher order that was discussed above. If an enemy of greater stature than Marsile is required by God and Charlemagne it is essentially because, after a certain point, the character of the drama has changed. Roland determines the change when he sounds the oliphant and shows that he understands the meaning of his sacrifice. Thus Baligant's sudden arrival can occur only after his death. Our poet thinks and works with enough vitality to substantiate such an explanation.

The fact remains that the Baligant episode is distinctly less concise than the first two parts of the *Chanson*, less firm in its balance of psychological elements. The initial effect is somewhat irritating, but it would be a great mistake to rest with that impression. In a struggle between incompatible worlds, individuals must give way to the causes they defend. The psychological realism of the prologue has to be followed by a progressively abstract and ideological concern. The old emperor now bears the overwhelming burden of his lofty mission alone. Of course the fact that he has to perform Roland's role as well as his own lends him youth and unexpected energy. But, for the most part, he receives his spirit and confidence by convincing himself of the nobility of his cause. Before he undertakes the great duel with Baligant, he repeats over and over, "I have justice on my side." Again God must help him directly or put him in the care of an angel — but the supernatural belongs here. This last battle is more God's than it is Charlemagne's.

Because the Baligant episode differs from what has gone before, then, it reveals the poet's intelligence and sensitivity. His genius is ready to confront any difficulty. If he ever achieves the sublime, it is in describing Roland's death. But he has demanded so much of this death that he should not now relax his effort. His inspiration does not fail him.

That the *Chanson* follows a perfectly logical course to its end can be demonstrated in another way. With Roland gone, Charlemagne assumes the central position in the narrative. Some arguments claim that this unavoidable change compromises the unity of the work: they can be refuted. If Roland is dead, he is no less involved in the action. Everything that happens in the second part of the poem is because of him and for him. It hardly seems necessary to repeat that, if the drama has been elevated, it is because Roland's sacrifice has taken on the dignity of martyrdom. Furthermore, it has been clear from the start that Charlemagne is on a different plane from his nephew. Although the emperor is not immune to anxiety and sorrow, he is above human passions. His majesty keeps him from the front of the stage. Attention focuses on Roland because he speaks and acts, and must be more directly answerable for Roncevaux. In the Baligant episode, the wise old man is not usurping a role that does not belong to him. He remains apart, although circumstances bring him closer to us. They pull him from his isolation and force him to act directly. Far from eclipsing his nephew or his memory, Charlemagne risks losing something of his own superhuman grandeur.

But the poet knows that to avenge Roland and reveal the full meaning of his death is a task for Charlemagne alone. As the young hero's destiny, so poignant in itself, is fulfilled, the author is careful to stress that this destiny is the vital, concrete symbol of the huge struggle that Charlemagne has been charged by God to wage. Through both memory and example, Roland becomes all the more important. He thus emphasizes the nobility of the cause guarded by the emperor. There is no danger of uncle and nephew obstructing one another. Charlemagne avenges Roland: Roland remains the character around whom the work is organized but, in pursuing his vengeance, Charlemagne retains the dignity of his sacred mission. Through his tribute Charlemagne elevates Roland and does not debase himself. We are not dealing with a *Chanson de Charlemagne* grafted onto a *Chanson de Roland*. We have, rather, a *Roland* that is carried from drama to myth by a powerful inspiration. Charlemagne belongs in this lofty region. Yet Roland joins him, and leads us there as well. With its skillful balance and ordered development, our poem once again refutes its critics.

We must now return to the specifics of the Baligant episode. We have already discussed the emir's arrival and sudden alteration of the course of events. His arrival does not actually compound the old emperor's task. Since Marsile and Baligant are allied, it is the same battle for Charles, although it has assumed gigantic proportions. It is appropriate that the second battle at Roncevaux should be a continuation of the first, and deliver Saragossa and her dying king to the conqueror, while assuming the magnitude demanded by Roland's martyrdom and Charlemagne's character, the poet realized this and, in carrying it out, put his merits as an architect to a new test. The plot takes shape at Saragossa, and the attack on Roland is launched from there. Baligant receives Marsile's homage at Saragossa and agrees to continue the war. When Baligant and the hapless king are dead, the people of Saragossa can only choose between death and conversion. But it is at Roncevaux that the decisive action occurs and the meaning emerges. Roland dies; Charlemagne triumphs.

Another noteworthy aspect of the symmetry is the role of Queen Bramidoine, first when Baligant arrives and later when his defeat is announced. Also important is the contrast on the day after the first battle between the deep sorrow of the French at Roncevaux as they bury their dead and the rage of the pagans at Saragossa, who insult their idols. The author is faithful to such simple and effective methods, which he uses each time with great effect. We certainly find them working in the description of the second battle. The poet always enjoys describing assembled armies, single combat, and the various outcomes. There is a risk here of repetition and monotony, but instead he manages to be both graphic and exciting. The poet juggles contrasts for the vital effect, admitting traces of irony and exoticism. Most admirable is his presentation of the great duel between Charlemagne and Baligant. The two adversaries dominate the other combatants in both size and majesty, their struggle symbolizing all the others. They are the living images of the two religions that confront each other at this decisive moment. Thus the quiet presence of an angel at Charlemagne's side seems quite natural. The two battles at Roncevaux and the outcomes must be parallel, the connection between them clear. An ordinary talent could not create and satisfy such demands.

Ganelon's trial has not aroused the same objections as has the Baligant episode. It is more predictable. Because of its concise and realistic quality, it seems closer to the first part of the work. It takes us from the mythic level, to which the poet's imagination has led us, back to earth and to men. But we should not be deceived by appearances, for we are certainly not dealing with an ordinary judgment or punishment. Research has shown that the poet did not confine himself to contemporary custom in his description of the trial, particularly the judicial combat. He has obviously selected the most extreme punishment, since nothing else seems sufficiently cruel or degrading. Most curious is the fact that all the relatives and friends who agreed to act as Ganelon's guarantees are put to death along with him. Medieval justice never went that far. These are liberties that even poetry would not take without good reason. Our author's reasons were excellent, as a literal reading will show. With firm pride Ganelon maintains that, since he was deeply insulted, he had the right to avenge himself and that he cannot be accused of treason because he challenged his stepson publicly. His position seems so logically strong that the council is almost unanimous in considering his acquittal. His death would deprive the empire of a powerful baron; it would not bring Roland back to life. Thierry alone approaches the indignant emperor and offers to uphold his accusation by arms. "Whatever wrong Roland may have done Ganelon," he says, "his service to you should guarantee him. Ganelon is the criminal . . . it is you he forswore and betrayed."

During the duel between Thierry and Pinabel, the poet goes so far as to tell us that God knows what the outcome will be. He makes it clear that Ganelon's crime affects not only the nephew and vassal but also the uncle and lord; not only the saint and martyr but also the head of Christendom, Christendom itself, and even God. He clearly states that as God miraculously intervened when Roland was about to die and when Charlemagne was at grips with Baligant, so will he intervene a third time to help the champion of his cause; to the weaker Thierry he grants the victory Pinabel thought was his. Answering Charlemagne's prayer, he makes "justice shine out." But the duel is long and bitter, for there is no victory here or in heaven without effort, pain, and sacrifice.

This, then, is the overarching law that governs the poem's inspiration, its epic and religious impulse. Ganelon ignores and misunderstands the law to his own arrogant ends, and he deserves death: a death that truly kills since it touches his soul and commits it to eternal damnation. Roland accepts the law when he urges the French, who are drawn to Marsile's offer, to carry on the holy war, the war that must never be interrupted and that cannot end. He courageously submits to the law when he falls at Roncevaux, and his salvation is all the more glorious since he perishes only because of his great sorrow and effort. When Charlemagne, despite his great age, confronts Baligant in the front ranks of the French, he fulfills his awesome obligation to the law. So does the beautiful Aude when she dies, an innocent victim, overcome like Roland by the enormity of her grief; and so does Thierry when he answers Pinabel's challenge and fights to the limit of his endurance. The *Chanson* would not be complete without evoking this law in an ultimate vision. In the aftermath of the battle the old emperor seeks his due repose, as did Vigny's Moses: the angel Gabriel visits him in his sleep and tells him that new trials await him. "God," he sighs, "how painful my life is!" But he knows he will answer this new command from heaven because his mission as leader and his situation as a man demand it.

Pauphilet has said that the *Chanson de Roland* is one of the best-constructed poems in the world. He is right, and we might add that its construction depends upon a classic simplicity and economy. From the first verse to the last, with a splendid crescendo of ominous reverberations, each scene is linked, and its arrangement conditioned, by a theme both epic and religious:

heroic sacrifice and redemptive suffering. A single atmosphere pervades the entire narrative. It clarifies the initial situation, explains the drama's origin, its development and meaning. Of course the emotions of the protagonists provoke the catastrophe and make it inevitable — as in the great French tragedies, the forces behind the action are essentially phychological. But if the characters engage in combat and, no matter how free, feel fatally impelled, it is because they do not make a sufficiently high ideal of the Crusade and its obligations. The battle that resolves this conflict decides not only the fate of Roland and Ganelon; it reveals the value of the great principles, or rather of the ideal, that the unrestrained passions of these men have threatened. The scheme of the drama changes and is no longer just a feud. It has acquired a much greater significance. The twofold conclusion emphasizes its scope and aspirations, implied from the start by the dominant theme.

The poem is classic not only in structure and aims, but also because of the author's craft. Inspiration submits to reason to the last detail. Effects are calculated with extreme care: suggestions, echoes, parallels and contrasts, repetitions and gradual progressions allow the poet to unfold situations, events, and their consequences with restraint as well as power. This skill greatly enhances the effect of his poetry. He regulates and amplifies the flights of spirit and imagination rather than stifling them. He is selective, not acquisitive, about his resources. He controls the mechanisms set in motion, using significant ellipses whose implications are easily grasped. The poetry invites effort from the reader, and the effort is always rewarded. Through his sense of timing and tact, the poet avoids artificiality and banality. Since it is so sure, it hardly matters whether this intelligence is more instinctive than conscious. Nor must we see it as more intricate than it is, or as too simple or schematic. It would be a mistake to rely on rigid logic to criticize certain choices or speak of errors, deficiencies, and interpolations. To suppose, as some have, that the poem makes frequent use of some sort of numerical symbolism is also a mistake. There seems little point in overlooking accessible beauty in order to search for secrets that may not exist. Unequivocal pleasure is surely preferable to illusive or uncertain satisfaction.

We have affirmed the unity of the *Chanson de Roland* while refuting the various criticisms of its structure. The impulse to gamble may have been a motive here, and it should now be clear that this is the kind of bet there is a chance of winning — to return to Bédier's word, an initial *précellence* suggests others, and the preceding pages have confirmed this expectation. If our confidence in the architectural ability of the *Roland* poet has been satisfied, let us now turn to his portrayal of character.

SEVEN · THE PORTRAYAL

OF CHARACTER

The preceding study of composition and meaning of the *Roland* is an important step toward an understanding of the characters whose fates are decided at Roncevaux. As Faral has so aptly stated, "Ideas are the vital principle of the *Chanson*, but the poetic force and moral beauty of these ideas are revealed only through the characters." He is right: in the poem, men control the action and problems are posed through character studies. The author, resolving his difficulties with ease, creates figures who are both vital and representative, real and epic. This applies in particular to those who enjoy his solicitude and admiration. Let us begin by discussing Roland.

As early as the council scene, the character of the hero is clearly defined by several brief remarks. He speaks first, to gain the advantage. He rejects all compromise and denies fatigue. "Lay siege [to Saragossa]", he says to Charlemagne, "though it last all your life." Roland understands the situation and is positing a principle. But he is also revealing his temperament. A word from Oliver, which foreshadows the later debate with Roland, confirms this: when Roland offers to bear the peace offering to Marsile, Oliver appeals to him directly. "You should certainly not go . . . your nature is too fierce and proud. I fear you would get into a fight."

The sketch soon becomes more detailed and precise. Roland is both courageous and generous. He is always ready to fight, a warrior to the end. He is also a vassal, devoted in soul and body to his lord and uncle, Charlemagne. He exceeds the emperor's expectations and, sparing nothing, has conquered province after province, kingdom after kingdom. Honor is his great concern. Above all he fears failure, in his own eyes or in the opinion of his peers. He would a thousand times die rather than see his reputation and his glory suffer. Unfortunately he is too much aware of his worth, too concerned with his own exploits. Even when he bids farewell to his sword, at the very moment of death, he reveals a substantial element of personal satisfaction. If Durendal is so beautiful and holy, it must be because of the noble vassal by whose mighty arm it was wielded. In such a situation it is rather inappropriate for Roland to congratulate himself like this. He also reveals his extreme conceit when he compares the valorous blows of others, particularly Oliver, to his own. In the midst of battle he cries, "My friend is angry; [such blows] are as good as mine!" We know that this ungovernable pride is even more responsible for Roncevaux than Ganelon's hatred. Certainly there are challenges that must be met, especially when they also constitute a tribute, and honor demands that Roland accept with pride a post reserved for the most courageous. But he is unwise to reject reinforcements. His refusal to summon Charlemagne when Marsile appears is not heroism but presumption, even audacious vanity. Intoxicated by success, a slave to the admiration of which he is the object, Roland assumes the gravest responsibilities at the risk of endangering all he hopes to save.

Ganelon is all too familiar with Roland's propensity to combine scorn with self-assurance and spite with irony. It drives him to revenge and treason. On the other hand, the deepest affections and the most vital, generous emotions are concentrated upon Roland: the old emperor's love for his nephew, Oliver's devotion to his inseparable friend, the admiration of the French for their famous chief who leads them to victory and spoils. Roland is worthy of these feelings because he can return them. He fights not only for himself, but for his lord, for France, for all Christendom. If he is too proud, it is for the honor of all that he loves and defends without regard for his own pain or life. His companions in arms pay him a magnificent tribute when they accept death at his side; he responds with the sincerity of his admiration, the depth of his gratitude, and the enormity of his suffering.

In Roland personal weaknesses are combined with the finest qualities. Far from disturbing the unity of his character, these weaknesses humanize him. The poet understood this much; he also knew that it is not enough to describe the qualities on which the morality of human beings depends. He must also show how a man fulfills his destiny, changes and yet is the same man, and achieves or falls short of salvation. Thus the drama of Roncevaux is essentially the story of a spirit that repents. Roland advocates a struggle to the end; he suspects certain men of affected weariness; he offers to bear Charlemagne's note to Saragossa; he braves an unequal fight and resolutely intensifies his efforts — these deeds reveal the best part of his heroism. But he also insults and enrages Ganelon; he refuses Oliver's advice; unmindful of the pagan hordes, he undertakes a battle whose outcome should have been clear to him — these actions reflect the worst part of his pride. The terrible result is that, through his only flaw, Roland provokes the treason. In the preceding pages I have referred to this flaw as *démesure*, rashness. In its extreme form it has been condemned by writers in the past not only because it involves the overthrow of reason, but because it is a rejection of the human condition, even a rebellion of man against God. Whatever we may reproach Roland for, it is clear that he does not go this far. He is the victim of his excessive virtues and his intentions are good. This is why he catches himself and, without denying his nature, finds the motive and the means for repentance. The extreme of heroic sacrifice cannot alone offset his pride; he must understand suffering, forget himself for his men, reveal a little humility. He faints as he sees his men fall around him; he dreads the loss of the battle he was sure of winning; he fears for Charlemagne, France, and Christianity. Finally he decides to sound the oliphant. Insofar as he has to be pardoned, this act, no act of despair but as much a prayer as a call for help, saves him.

Some critics have gone so far as to say that in the poet's eyes Roland is never wrong because there is no heroism without a kind of divine madness, before which reason and wisdom must bow. All things considered, this opinion and the preceding analysis are not irreconcilable. In writing a *chanson de geste*, Turoldus could not confine his interest to Roland's personal destiny. He had to put his epic genius to the test and create people who were also examples and symbols. Roland embodies a theology that includes militant faith, nascent patriotism, chivalric honor, and belligerent heroism. This same spirit led Christian and feudal society of the eleventh century to undertake the grandiose enterprise of the Crusades. Roland is motivated by the same powerful forces that drew together huge crowds and inspired incredible feats. His character has to include all these factors, and yet he cannot become an inhuman, theoretical ideal. In fact he does not have to deny himself in order to become a model, for his personal virtues and faults can only incite him to make the crusading spirit his own. He is vital and real, as much because of his ideals as his temperament. Both parts blend in him, and are fitting. The extremes of his nature find their justification in the grandeur of his ideals. Although Roland sets himself off from the common man, his nobility and his extremism make him the representative of an entire epoch, and this is the measure of the poet's skill. He has made of Roland an epic character who is both individual and representative, resolving the contradiction that was just encountered in our discussion of his rashness and his redemption.

Roland is merciless in battle, and his heroism is unlimited. As I have said, he risks harm to the very interests he wishes to serve. But the total sacrifice to which he is led offsets the fatal effects that his extreme audacity and concern for honor might have produced. Nothing could better ensure the success of Roland's cause than such a sacrifice. It is the most striking proof of the nobility of that cause; it revives weakened spirits, makes revenge an obligation, and fixes the price that must be paid. In a word, it introduces the element of duty. Though he is responsible for Roncevaux, Roland deserves the finest death and the highest reward, for sacrifice is not in vain, nor ambition wrong, when one is fighting for God and Christianity. But since his first impulse was not entirely pure, Roland must be the first to learn from the great example that his death is soon to offer others. The gift he is finally able to make includes not only his bravery and his life, but his egotism and his audacity. The price is high, but it frees him from regret for his acts and allows him to die both victorious and serene. Because he responds to the appeal of grace, his madness surpasses wisdom, and unites with holiness. The blood that is shed because of this madness is not a symbol of defeat and death. Like that of the martyrs, it promises the resurrection of the soul and the triumph of faith. Critics of this interpretation should remember that whatever takes Roland's earthly life also opens wide to him the gates of eternal life. His skin is untouched by Saracen weapons; he dies by his own generous, painful effort — which burst his temples.

No one will deny that such a death fulfills a Christian ideal, though perhaps the example is so noble as to discourage imitation. But despite its epic and spiritual austerity, Roland's sacrifice involves a man who is very much of this world. A detail, often overlooked, emphasizes this fact: as the hero is dying, he beats his breast with one hand and with the other holds his glove toward God. Oliver has died as a soldier, Turpin as a prelate. Roland links the Christian act with that of the vassal. These subtle points answer a specific need: according to the poet, any expression of religious sentiment, no matter how exalted, must take a feudal and chivalric form. To be disturbed by this would be a mistake. As the Grail literature shows, such a transposition reflects one of the most characteristic tendencies of the medieval spirit, which was anxious to reconcile the demands of Christianity and of social morality. Imagery borrowed from contemporary institutions and life was adapted to evangelical teaching, without the least sacrilegious intent. Quite the opposite: the purpose was to make Christianity closer and more immediate and, at the same time, to give chivalry a deep religious significance. This attempt to unite, at the highest level of awareness, a truth revealed by God and an ideal constructed by man is both beautiful and moving. And it is certainly natural in a time when, without losing his old identity, the vassal-turned-crusader was transformed into a soldier of Christ and entrusted with the very destiny of Christianity.

In this way our poet stayed in close contact with his readers without sacrificing his high ideals. Roland assumes the attitude of a penitent when he offers his glove to God, but he does not forget that he is a knight. Even as he is leaving the world, he shows how much he is still attached to it. Without this gesture, and the sentiment it reflects, Roland's death would be less moving — and also less significant. What is admirable in leaving something without regret? Roland is fully aware of all the reasons he has to live. He mourns his youth, his friendships, his conquests, his glory. He is sorrowful but not bitter as he looks at his faithful sword and thinks of Charlemagne and fair France. He had already been redeemed by pain when he sounded the oliphant: the pain of a hero acknowledging his limits and his defeat. Yet his last words express the simple sadness of a man who is going to die. The hero's humility is pleasing to God, but we are much closer to the man's sorrow. Through the man we can better understand the hero, for the most lowly achieve salvation just as the saints do. The form of the test may vary; it can be more or less severe, demanding different degrees of courage and endurance, deserving a greater or lesser reward. But if the form changes according to circumstance and character, its nature does not change. It is always proportionate to ability, always accompanied by an appeal to grace. It demands a free and absolute gift of the self. When sin is recognized, it is deprived of its force and becomes the incentive and basis for exoneration. Once accepted, goodness bursts forth unrestrained. Man and hero unite in the martyr of Roncevaux to provide a single example. However exceptional it may be, it is accessible to all because there is only one way to be saved.

In humanizing Roland the poet brings him closer to us, but his integrity is not damaged, nor his prowess and holiness diminished. Perhaps in the end it is the man who arises and saves the hero. One thing is certain: we recognize ourselves in him, and thus the message he bears, which is important to us all, gains in effect and validity. It is doubtful that the epic has ever again reached such heights, or that poet and character have ever been so ideally suited. And our admiration need not stop here, for the author of the *Chanson* did not exhaust his genius with Roland.

Pauphilet has described Oliver as an "insubstantial character, defined only along general moral lines and created only for the sake of a magnificent and short-lived literary effect." This is true enough, as far as it goes. But does Oliver exist only to provide contrast to Roland's character? Is he no more than a useful figure of comparison? The fact is that Oliver is very much alive and at times even becomes the center of attention and sympathy.

His wisdom is evident from his first words, when he offers to carry Charlemagne's note and rebukes Roland for his fierce and proud heart. Thus the wisdom he shows at Roncevaux is no surprise. He is the first to understand the extent of the danger and to see the treason. He realizes immediately that to summon Charlemagne is not cowardice but duty. He is wiser than Roland, but no less brave. Since he does not share his comrade's confidence in an impossible victory, and foresees the outcome of the battle, he is all the more noble for fighting like a hero, urging the French on, tireless himself to the very end. "A curse on the slowest!" he cries, charging the enemy. And the pagan who deals him a mortal blow from behind speaks this fine elegy: "In you alone I have avenged all our men."

With his intelligence and courage Oliver is also a perfect friend. He is modest and self-effacing with Roland, and without envy. As he is dying he doubtless feels the cruelty of a death that could have been avoided. But if he finds it hard to keep from overwhelming Roland with reproaches that are only too justified, he yearns with all his heart for reconciliation; he needs it if he is to die in peace. The balanced union of perfection and humanity lends sorrow and pathos to Oliver's noble figure. Created for Roland, he has everything to lose from this comparison and might have been as abstract as the contrast from which he has emerged. But the poet makes him love, and even lets us harbor a secret preference for him. Thus Oliver becomes a surprisingly vital character.

The poet has been equally successful in making Oliver an epic figure. To this end he has made use of a theme that stems both from eleventh-century feudal life and from the Virgilian tradition: the warrior companionship. Before their military apprenticeship, certainly from the first moment of taking up arms and for some time thereafter, the young "bachelors" of the Middle Ages had to share the same education, pleasures, and trials. Roland and Oliver owe their deep friendship to this communal life, and Roland's love for the beautiful Aude makes the bond even more fraternal. They are not the only knights to share this bond. Other warrior companions, whose very names may be similar, will meet the same fate as Roland and Oliver at Roncevaux or, in other works, evoke their memory: Ami and Amile, Gerin and Gerier, Lancelot and Galahad. But it is in the *Chanson* that this common bond, so effectively revived, reveals its poetic strength and assumes its greatest significance. In fact, the poet prolongs the expected parallel by creating an unexpected conflict. The quarrel between Oliver and Roland is moving because it involves two men who are equally generous, equally ready for sacrifice, and very eager to understand one another. The collision of the two perspectives is the more startling because it throws both moral attitudes into question, and calls on us to judge them. Will we, like the poet, choose Roland's prowess over Oliver's wisdom? We know that Roland's cause demands an unlimited and tireless effort. The boldest sacrifice serves it better than timely prudence or the cleverest strategy. An irrational gesture is expected of the greatest champions, a true passion that culminates in martyrdom. Redeemed by the virtue of suffering, passion and martyrdom justify audacity and transform earthly defeat into a spiritual victory and a redemptive example. Oliver is able to accept both passion and martyrdom, and even to make an offering of them. But he also questions their expediency, if not their nobility. His vision and logic are only those of human wisdom. He does not understand the supreme call of the oliphant any more than he accepted its silence. Most simply, between Oliver and Roland lies the gulf that separates the just man from the saint. One adjusts his acts to the simple demands of duty and, in excess, sees only folly and pride; the other believes that he is always acting for what God demands and desires. Oliver will be saved, but in heaven, even more than among the French, he will yield first place to Roland. Can he even aspire to second place?

The archbishop Turpin also has a claim to it. His character is striking, even surprising. He wants martyrdom to come when he has his sword drawn and is surrounded by foes who have fallen by his hand. Yet he does not renounce his role as priest. When the battle begins, he urges the French on with religious encouragements: he grants them absolution and recalls the sacred mission they must fulfill. When the battle is at its height and the outcome is clear, he again intervenes to explain the certainty both of their death and of their redemption. Finally, scarcely conscious himself, he solemnly blesses the dead and tries to relieve Roland's thirst: this act of reassurance and pity exhausts his final breath. Could his priesthood have a more worthy end? Since he is a good archbishop, Turpin is not required to excel as a knight. Should we reproach him for wanting to be both, when his companions and the poet praise him for it? We ought rather to recognize that he belongs to an age in which religious enthusiasm demands action. Circumstance is the ruling factor. A crusade is not a sermon, but a war in which prowess and sanctity converge and replace the apostolate. Turpin has no choice when confronted with these adversaries: they are hardened heretics, beyond conversion, who must be dispatched to Satan with a brutal, resolute blow of the sword. Perhaps an archbishop ought to prefer a different approach. But Turpin fights with a good-natured frankness that, among the soldiers, can only assure his authority and augment his prestige. When he volunteers for the peace mission he says, "I would like to see what this Marsile looks like." And he comments on Roland's exploits as an expert: "That is the kind of courage a knight must have. Otherwise he is not worth a farthing and would be better as a monk, praying every day for our sins." A revealing remark, which the French echo when they say, "En l'arcevesque est ben la croce salve" (the crosier is certainly safe with the archbishop).

With his contrasts and his pride, Turpin is, like Roland and Oliver, at once real and exemplary. Faral writes that "his exploits symbolize the active faith, rich in deeds, which establishes the kingdom of God on earth while serving Christendom." Even beyond this, Turpin personifies the mystique of the Crusade in a particularly apt way. The Christian and chivalric ideals are perfectly united in him: how could this combination be better realized than in a champion of both man and God, a sword in one hand and a cross in the other? This is no poetic dream, for the ranks in both Spain and the East were soon to grow in their number of soldier-monks. By creating a character who responds so perfectly to the contemporary and future demands of the Crusades, the *Roland* poet again shows his epic genius. He shows it in still another way by infusing both the Crusade and the motive for his own inspiration with an element of French patriotism. It is no coincidence that Turpin is archbishop of Reims, the coronation city. From the center of Christianity he can better affirm the superiority of France and her king.

But titles cannot make Turpin Roland's equal. If military heroism is the best proof of faith, it seems natural that the most Christian of knights would surpass the most valiant of priests. We should not be surprised if sainthood is reserved for the man who has, even in rashness, best responded to the expectations and grace of God. Because of his rashness, Roland cannot be surpassed in battle. And because this same excess makes his martyrdom all the more painful, he is able to offer God a gift that neither Oliver's wisdom nor Turpin's stalwart serenity can equal. It demands greater merit, and thus promises greater glory.

This glory provides a contrast by which to measure Ganelon's guilt. In the course of the drama we have come to know Ganelon and are aware that he is anything but an ordinary traitor. He is a Christian, clever and thoughtful, valiant and protective of his honor. He enjoys the esteem of the French, and the advice he offers at Charlemagne's council is wise: he gains almost unanimous support. But he is too susceptible to the more tender emotions, to weariness, and to a deeply implanted bitterness. Is this enough to explain why he dares to commit the greatest of crimes?

His damnation is no more certain than Roland's redemption. The cause and the stages of Ganelon's fall are clear. In pointing them out, the poet does not diminish them; his perspective is that of a psychologist who understands his patient but remains objective. He realizes that a violent shock is necessary if Ganelon's destiny is suddenly to be altered. But he also sees that, for full effect, the shock must be prepared for. The anger and hatred released in Ganelon are old: long accumulated and long repressed, they burst out like a flood that sweeps all barriers before it. We witness the abdication of a conscience, paralyzed and helpless, which allows passion to think, will, and act in its place. Aided by the forces, both good and bad, that it enlists, this passion soon extends and compounds its havoc. Initially anxious, Ganelon grows impatient, sharpens and goads his anxiety, looks for motives, assumes new risks. In his imagination he already enjoys his triumph; through rationalization he justifies it and, through his will and intelligence, makes sure it will succeed. For an instant of evil joy, he yields to his passion and sacrifices all. And Ganelon, the respectable and respected baron, becomes the most odious of criminals. In the end he is overcome by the riches and the embraces he accepts, as well as by the same cool shrewdness and courage he uses to effect his insidious design.

Yet Ganelon is free. If he could have restrained his hatred, the intervention of divine grace would still have been possible. The chance is offered as soon as he voices his anger at Roland's choice. His attitude, and even his words, still contain enough nobility to make his damnation seem uncertain. He could have emphatically refuted his stepson by fulfilling his mission with dignity. This would have been sufficient vengeance for an honorable man, and Ganelon could have chosen it. He is still free to choose when, before his departure for Saragossa, he takes leave of his men. Their affection and esteem should help him to regain his self-control rather than feed his rancor. Later, in Marsile's camp, Ganelon defies the pagans even more resolutely than Roland would have, and is farther than ever from damnation. He has just proven his own strength to himself, a strength that can and ought to overcome hatred and evil. Do Marsile's riches and embraces give a better taste to the treason or a greater value to Roland's betrayal? In eliciting disgust they should have counteracted Ganelon's recent anger and fear. But he does not seize this final opportunity and, with his last excuse, loses his last chance.

Ganelon's most serious offense, perhaps, is that he is rational. He cannot but know that his plan will help the enemy as well as himself, that through Roland he affects Charlemagne and Christianity. But to justify himself he invokes the higher interests of the French and the Empire: all these wars of conquest are devastating; to kill those who prosecute them would be a good deed. Of course he is not really thinking of peace and war. The ambush at Roncevaux will bring up all the old problems and provoke new bloodshed. To him it makes no difference. Whether he admits it or not, the only thing he cares about is Roland's death, even if the world must suffer for it or if he must die soon after. It is all that can interest him now; everything else is insignificant in comparison. He wants it, at whatever price, because his hatred demands it and in his challenge he pledged it.

As the trial at Aix shows, Ganelon's crime is the result of an error and a denial that are equally unpardonable. He has succeeded in convincing himself that his revenge is not treason. He cannot understand that a pact with Marsile has nothing to do with one man's resentment toward another; nor does he see that in betraying his stepson he is taking a stand against God. He commits this mortal sin because he wants to, although his past, his intelligence, and the esteem in which he is held should prevent him and do offer the chance to turn back. The selflessness and humility that save Roland could also save him. But where pride is finally flexible, hatred is obdurate. Between the two attitudes lies an abyss, which separates sanctity from evil, the brilliant summits of paradise from the darkest depths of hell.

The figure of Charlemagne has still to be discussed. Of all the characters created by the Roland poet, his is certainly the most extraordinary. With its superhuman proportions the figure might have suffered from this very grandeur and, in dominating the drama, remained distant and indistinct. Actually Charles is no less vigorous or vital than the others. He is complex, subtle, intensely alive in his symbolic majesty.

Charles is not an abstract figure, invulnerable and inaccesible. He seems a little overwhelmed by his task, and labors under his heavy responsibilities to God and man. During the council scene he leaves the debate to the stormy barons; for the most part he is quiet, passive, and indecisive. Finally he has to be asked to impose silence, to give orders, and to exert his authority. Affection and gratitude dictate certain of his preferences. He owes so much to Roland that he excuses even his indiscretions, which irk some of the men; from Ganelon we know the extremes that can result from jealousy and bitterness. But though he has doubts and fears, the old king seems to have no defense against Roland's excesses. Charlemagne's suffering is the measure of his tenderness, as we see in his speech in the battlefield at Roncevaux:

> Friend Roland, valiant handsome youth, when I am at Aix, in my chapel, the vassals will come, seeking news. I will tell them, strange and dreadful . . . Ah! Sweet France, how empty you are. My sorrow is so great that I wish I were dead . . . Friend Roland, may God have mercy on you and place your soul in paradise! Whoever killed you has harmed all France. So great is my pain for the men who have died for me that I do not want to live. May God, the son of Saint Mary, grant that today, before I reach the main pass at Cize, my soul may be separated from my body, and placed among their souls, and my body buried next to theirs. (strophe 209)

And Charles's weariness on the eve of a life filled with trial and conflict is as human as his suffering: in the last lines of the poem the angel Gabriel comes to announce new hardships that await him, and Charles replies, "God, how painful my life is!" These weaknesses might have diminished Charlemagne's stature as hero and leader. But despite his characterization as a sensitive and good-natured old man, the great emperor can play only one role in the drama, the leading one. As Pauphilet points out, the subject and structure of the poem leave no doubt of this primacy. How has the poet achieved this effect without sacrificing either uncle or nephew?

Charlemagne's name is the first and the last to be mentioned in the *Chanson*. His character is immediately imposing: he is the silent focus of attention in the midst of the brilliant gathering of barons. We recognize him instinctively, and his sparsely drawn image remains etched in our memories. One might argue that he loses control of the events or that he is unable to alter their course. And indeed, until Roland's death, the old ruler is surprisingly passive. But we should not be deceived: the intricate drama and impending catastrophe affect his spirit far more deeply than they do any of the others. He doubts Marsile's good faith, mistrusts Ganelon's suggestions, and is visited by obscure but threatening dreams. He senses the inevitable but is unable to prevent it. This helpless anxiety certainly does not make him inferior to those who speak and act on emotion. It puts him in the background, but above the other characters. He alone understands the gravity of what has happened and of what lies ahead. As Pauphilet says, "this aspect of Charlemagne's character involves difficult compromises and decisions. The emperor could hardly witness such crucial events unmoved, but he must not be too knowledgeable or decisive: a word from him would destroy Ganelon's plot . . . and the very subject of the poem. The treason must succeed, but not at the expense of Charlemagne's foresight or authority. Hence these obscure warnings and partial visions, too vague to allow action, but strong enough to torment him." A better explanation than Pauphilet's would be impossible. In the first part of the *Chanson* it is Charlemagne's anguish that gives him stature. It allows him to be at the center of the drama without having provoked it, to experience it more completely, as both man and leader, than those who are acting it out. It confers on his role an incomparable tragic strength.

Charlemagne is not at the battle of Roncevaux, but the artist has turned his absence into an invisible presence. The French invoke Charlemagne before their charge, when they utter his war cry. Throughout the battle Charles' name is used both to praise and to insult, and the French willingly die at Roncevaux for all that the name represents. As the extent of the struggle and the sacrifices becomes apparent, it is increasingly clear that the emperor is the reason for it all. Even at a distance, he deeply feels the suffering and heroism of his men. On the return road his army is full of confident cheer; he is obsessed with forebodings that tie him to the battle. Again, the unhappy privilege of anguish reveals his lonely and exceptional grandeur. Even Roland's sacrifice enhances this grandeur, since it is an offering to the emperor. Then final actions and thoughts of the young hero show that, for him, everything begins and ends in Charlemagne. When Roland recalls his brief and glorious career, everything centers on the emperor: affection, honors, conquests. And his thoughts are of Charles as he sounds the oliphant. Does this mean that he owes to Charles his most sublime achievement, his very redemption? We can readily agree with Pauphilet's conclusion that "when Roland is dead and Charlemagne is alone in the foreground, the balance of the poem has not appreciably shifted: the emperor is hardly more the master, and Roland is hardly less alive . . . The second part of the *Chanson* does not alter Charlemagne's role, but exalts it."

Charlemagne plays this exalted role on the epic level as well as the dramatic. He certainly benefits from the bravery of his men and their sacrifices on his behalf. But he can profit from them only because he also is able to make sacrifices, though not every task is worthy of him. He saves himself for the highest ones, and thus is without equal. He surpasses even his nephew in the superhuman duel against Baligant and emerges as the living symbol of the Crusade. The poet has clearly described both the characters and the stakes in this venture, which mobilizes all Christianity in the service of God. He understands what the results can be when the desire for power, the chivalric mystique, and the new nationalism of a great people are combined with — and justified by — religious faith. But he is also able to transcend historical realities: the conflict between the West and Islam becomes a mythic struggle, without compromise or conclusion. Of course the description of the first day at Roncevaux must include precise details that locate it specifically in time and space, but, because of its implications, the battle ceases to be an isolated episode in any one crusade. By finally engaging all Christianity, it demands a revenge that is relevant to all crusades, past, present, and future. Charlemagne's presence allows this greater perspective. His personality is free of contingency; his army includes all the forces of the West; the beginning and end of his reign are unknown. Everything combines to make him an ideal sovereign. He is close to his men's hearts but admired for his exploits. The coronation has invested him with an element of divine power and made him the perfect king, an archetype. As interpreter for an entire people, the poet ennobles both Charlemagne's character and the mission with which he has been entrusted by depicting him in this way — and, in a most effective way, reveals the power and scope of his design.

The poet does run a risk: as both human and ideal, Charlemagne might seem to be the product of an impossible contradiction. But strength and weakness are natural in an old man. To his age Charles owes his fatigue, his misgivings, his thoughtfulness, and his sometimes slow wisdom. But to age he also owes his patriarchal solemnity and benevolence. Why should he be jealous of authority? For years he has found no egotistic satisfaction in the exercise of power. He knows that errors and injustices are easily committed. He surrounds himself with advisers and advice, and listens attentively, though his patience is sometimes tried. Charles weighs his decisions, confident of the respect he inspires: when the time comes, the French will understand and follow him. He also knows the extremes to which men can be driven by emotion, and fears these emotions all the more because of his long struggle to subdue his own. Because of his years of experience, his understanding, if imperfect, surpasses that of both youth and maturity. As a judge he is as fair and equitable as possible, but he often has to control his own feelings and susceptibilities. His past trials have not hardened him, but have only made him more sensitive to pain — his own as well as others'. Over the years he has certainly become aware of his enormous responsibilities. Never would he fail the mission with which he has been entrusted, but he suffers for it enough to be justified in feeling its weight, and this is why he counts on Roland's youthful vigor. When he is deprived of his best support, he must make a heroic effort to regain his strength. That effort allows him to perform wonders and revives the power of his fighting arm. We can be surprised by this only if we forget that, in the epic, the marvelous becomes credible. And, more than any other character in the *Chanson*, Charlemagne has the benefit of supernatural support.

As the leader of the Christian army he is, in effect, chosen by God. As we have noted, age modifies certain contradictions in his nature. It humanizes him and brings him closer to us — but it also separates him from this world. With his flowing beard, he has been the emperor for as long as men can remember: is he two hundred years old, as Marsile thinks? His age is like that of the great Old Testatment figures through whom the God of the Bible spoke and acted. Charlemagne's actions also contribute to this impression. When Marsile offers to convert, Charles lifts his hands in a gesture of prayer and gratitude. When he bids farewall to Ganelon, his ambassador, he blesses and absolves him with the sign of the Cross. To his temporal prerogatives are added sacramental and priestly powers. Turpin is both archbishop and knight: is Charles emperor and pope of Christianity as well? This is the poet's implication, but he is too subtle to insist on it. The emperor is a vital image of the militant Christianity of the Crusades, which in itself warrants the solicitude and intervention of divine power. Thus God suddenly appears to warn, inspire, protect, and save Charlemagne. On the eve of Roncevaux he sends Charles prophetic dreams. To allow Charlemagne to destroy Marsile's army he repeats the miracle granted to Joshua: he stops the sun and prolongs daylight. The next night he troubles Charles again with visions and marvels, and sends the angel Gabriel to his side. As we know, this holy messenger returns to help the old champion in his duel against Baligant and, at the end of the poem, conveys the order to raise new armies. God not only helps Charlemagne to conquer the emir of Babylon; he was also at Roncevaux to welcome Roland's soul and will be at Aix to help Thierry defeat Pinabel. He reveals himself at the three crucial moments of the drama, and each time it is in the emperor's behalf. Through Thierry — and even through Roland — God defends, honors, and vindicates Charlemagne: he owes all his favors to his chosen one, the head of Christendom. The supernatural manifestations, infrequent before Roland's death, become numerous and impressive after it. The hero of Roncevaux is dead and Charlemagne is alone in the face of his immense task, oppressed with grief, deprived of his best support. He has never deserved a miracle more. Can it be refused when the very circumstances demand it?

The poet should not be criticized for using the supernatural. He knows exactly what he is doing. It is not a question of literary artifice: Christian miracle is part of the reality that inspires the work, and so is more appropriate here than in any other epic. The eleventh-century crusaders were certain that they had God's support against the infidels; each of them felt, at some decisive moment, that he was part of a celestial army. The *Roland* poet knew this better than anyone. There are possible pitfalls, but he has avoided them. At first the supernatural is only implicit. We expect miracles and wonders in the *Chanson*, but they occur only in exceptional situations, to emphasize sublime nobility or spiritual significance. They are skillfully introduced and seem as natural as they are necessary. Often they take the form of a cautionary sign, but when a vision is involved, it is described with remarkable moderation and restraint. The angels who descend from heaven to welcome a soul or give a helpful warning are shadowy images, more suggestion than fact. That God does not appear is an artistic choice, not a sign of weakness. The *Roland* poet unites respect for God with a delicate literary sense; he knows that poetry can suffer from explicitness and thrives on suggestion.

Because he is adept at exploring the minds of his characters, the poet avoids other problems. In the *Chanson* the miraculous does not upset the natural order of things or interfere with the autonomy of the individual's moral life. Each man must determine the quality of his heroism and sacrifice, and bear full responsibility for his errors and faults. The dreams that come to Charlemagne are thus mysterious. Though frightening, they do not define the danger; the greatest intelligence could not foresee the imminent catastrophe. Whether he makes a decision or not, the emperor is completely free. His choice is not imposed on him. When God gives the victory to one of his favorites — Roland, Charlemagne, or Thierry — the situation is similar. These victories are unexpected, and thereby miraculous. Without divine aid they would have been impossible. But the merit of the three men is not diminished: they triumph because of their physical energy and spiritual strength. God confines himself to an encouraging word or sign. When Charlemagne begins to weaken, the angel Gabriel simply says, "Great King, what are you doing?" These words are all the old monarch needs to regain confidence in victory and strength to defeat his enemy. Though fleeting, the miraculous is the clear embodiment of an act of grace, a gesture that can be either answered or ignored. It does not force souls to save themselves against their will.

The drama at Roncevaux remains a human drama, created by passion, ruled by the characters. God changes nothing by revealing himself. But if he allows the characters to decide their fates, he does not lessen the brilliance of his own power, goodness, and justice. He gives meaning to the events and actions because, as he mysteriously directs them by his sovereign will, he no less mysteriously allows men a freedom by which they are ennobled without being deprived of his aid. The poet has been faithful both to human realities and to the message of the Gospel. Because of this delicate equilibrium he is able to create epic figures that would otherwise be missing from the literature of the world.

EIGHT · THE ART OF
THE POET

If art consists primarily of constructing and ordering a subject, of examining man and his fate, and of using realism to transcend reality, then the *Roland* poet clearly possesses all the elements that distinguish a great artist. But the greatest skill is worthless if it is unfulfilled. Both the form and the effect of our author's work must be studied.

As we know, the critics remained quite oblivious to the quality of the *Chanson* in the years following Francisque-Michel's edition (1837). Of course there was a reaction, but romanticism had a special way of admiring the Middle Ages. Thus Paul de Saint-Victor, with more enthusiasm than insight, exclaimed: "It is the infancy of art, but a herculean infancy that achieves the sublime in a single bound." Gustave Lanson's attitude, still fairly common today, is even more typical. In the first editions of

Littérature he wrote: "The characters are barbarous, violent, brutal, with poor, narrow brains almost devoid of ideas. Where is that marvelous flexibility and bright affluence of the Greek soul, even in the rugged times of the Homeric wars?" Although acknowledging a certain "dramatic intensity" in the verses of the Oxford text, he adds: "The absence of art, or an inadequate use of it, the contrast or disproportion between the simplicity of means and the fullness of effect, are responsible for the charm of popular poetry." Bédier found reason to reject this position. He claimed that the author of the *Roland* was not content merely to sing, but had to "sit down at his desk, search for combinations, effects, and rhymes, consider, arrange, and select. Poets today work in this way, and they always have. When they say that they sing as other men breathe, they are bragging, and whoever believes them is mistaken; they work; it is a craft to make a book . . . there is no other legitimate explanation for the creative process."

We shall now attempt our own conclusion. It should be no surprise that we have to cover old ground to do full justice to the *Roland* poet. Certain thought patterns and prejudices, romantic as well as classical, must be overcome. And to understand the various decisions of our author is not an easy task. We are dealing with a difficult, elliptical, unintellectual style. Faral notes that, although there is no lack of ideas in the poem, they are never expressed in abstract form but always "based on the concrete," expressed through images or acts. There is no explanation or commentary, not even a confidence to share, and this can be confusing. But this abrupt, intuitive compactness can be understood by those who are willing to make the effort.

Certain of these problems are not difficult to unravel. In our study of the poem's structure, we found that the author likes to establish parallels and contrasts between the various events of the story, and does it with great success. A good example is to be found in the two introductory scenes. Everything in Charlemagne's camp indicates victory, breathes of strength, youth, and loyalty. But in the midst of the luxury and ostentation that surround Marsile, anxiety and treachery prevail. That this is a simple contrast does not prevent this sequence from being the best of introductions. Without an extraneous word, it puts us *in media res*, defines the subject, establishes the characters, creates the atmosphere. The poet explains by example, wants the reader to understand by observation. There is no need to accumulate a list of instances, though many immediately come to mind. To speak of sparseness of monotony in the *Roland* would be fallacious. The poet never uses a formula mechanically. His contrasts and repetitions are never artificial because he scorns pat devices. Ganelon's selection as ambassador parallels Roland's assignment to the rear guard but, as one initiates the drama, the other effects the treason. Although they are both carried out in the same terms, Roland, in his maliciousness, is quick and spontaneous. Ganelon's act is premeditated, the result of treacherous calculation. This distinction is a master stroke in a carefully conceived and brilliantly applied plan.

The very development of the drama demands parallels and contrasts to reveal minds and emotions, to explain both the origin and the progress of the action. The painful argument that twice opposes Roland and Oliver during the battle provides a good example. Roland finally accepts what he first rejected because something has changed in his soul, and his vision is greater. But Oliver does not change. He contradicts his previous counsel because he now sees no hope of averting the disaster. Human logic and wisdom are insufficient to explain the deed that saves Roland. There is no point in treating it as an ordinary event.

There are other examples of this artistry. Before the first

battle, the poet compares Marsile's twelve peers to Charlemagne's. And before the final encounter between the emperor and Baligant, he compares the battalions of the French and the Saracen armies. This technique is as old as the epic itself; the question is whether it is being used in a new way. Certainly the Christians present a magnificent spectacle; the procession of the hundred thousand barons of France is particularly admirable. On the other hand, the description of the infidels, with its accumulation of strange names, seems an exaggeration if not a caricature. Still, the author who has unleashed this avalanche of characters knows that the epic demands overstatement. For him, the war that opposes the armies of Charles and Baligant represents a mythic struggle between the forces of good and evil, between God's elect and the followers of the devil. One has to consider the full horror of the danger at the moment that the decisive battle begins, when the epic tension must be brought to its peak. The poet should hardly be reproached for trying to rise to the grandeur of his subject. It is more relevant to point out that his strident, colorful descriptions are exciting and effective for their exotic as well as their humorous touches.

Just as he knows how to use parallels and contrasts, the author of the *Roland* understands the importance of thematic ground-work. We are familiar with the role played by the theme of French weariness throughout the *Chanson*. It accounts for Blancandrin's offers and the debate they provoke. It explains the conflict that erupts between Roland and Ganelon, and enhances the significance of both Roland's rashness and Ganelon's weakness, clarifying the argument of one and the protestations of the other. This same theme reappears when, because of Roland's death, Charlemagne is left alone to face Baligant. And the last lines of the poem echo it, when the angel Gabriel comes to impose new trials on the old emperor, who longs for repose. The

cautionary dreams and omens that suddenly threaten danger
or imminent catastrophe could hardly be more skillful or
striking. Is the poet's use of this groundwork so heavy-handed
as to prevent any element of the unexpected? We know that he
does not deserve this reproach. He is interested not in surprise
but in pathos; he wants his listeners and characters to live the
drama of Roncevaux. The characters can do so only if they
have forebodings, and the listeners only if they know or suspect
the outcome. Emotion is possible only when curiosity gives way
to fear of the inevitable. It takes more than talent to meet
such demands successfully.

The absence of surprise in the narrative is easily offset by the
fact of its progressive intensity, which gives an unexpected
perspective and meaning to events, even if they are formally
announced or seem inevitable. This is nowhere better illustrated
than in the last episodes of the battle, when Oliver, Turpin, and
then Roland fall. These deaths, so close yet so different, form a
hierarchy based on the degree and scope of each sacrifice. Here
we can discern not only the preferences of the poet, but also
the underlying reasons that explain and justify them. Rather
than restating these reasons, we shall quote Pauphilet, who shows
in a particularly apt way the degree of perfection that the poet
can achieve:

> Three times . . . Roland tries in vain to break his sword,
> and three times he marvels at it lovingly. The sword also
> has its agony, and must remain unconquered and intact to
> the end. Just as no one can wound Roland, no one can mar
> the steel of the sword. The poet has marked these attempts
> in three symmetrical and distinct *laisses*, where, characteris-
> tically, the developing ideas combine with echoes of what has
> gone before. When Roland speaks to his sword in the first

and shortest *laisse*, he calls it only "good and unfortunate," expresses his sorrow, and recalls the victories gained with the sword. In the second *laisse*, Durendal is "beautiful and bright"; Roland compares its brilliance to the sun, and mentions its divine origin . . . In the third, Durendal is "most holy"; the memories of glory and conquest are replaced by a description of the famous relics in the handle. The praise becomes increasingly exalted; the weapon of war becomes a holy weapon, almost a symbol. And similarly the life of the hero, which seems to have been evoked by the weary thoughts of a dying man, slowly changes and is idealized. Roland was truly the soldier of God. (*Le Legs du moyen âge*, p. 85)

A poet has to be judged by his use of the available means of expression. The author of the *Roland* does not strictly depend on the most used forms of traditional rhetoric, but no one knows better than he how to make them effective by intelligent artistic handling.

A narrative is valuable not only for its organization and execution, but also for the way in which it is illustrated. Our poet describes in order to explain, but he does so with surprising restraint and admirable economy. The two contrasting scenes that serve as introduction to the poem again come to mind, particularly the second, rich in color and movement:

The emperor is in a broad orchard, and with him are Roland and Oliver, the Duke Sansun, and the proud Anseis, and Gefrey of Anjou, the King's standard-bearer. Gerin and Gerer are with him also, and many others. There are fifteen thousand from sweet France. The knights are seated on white silk carpets. The clever and the elderly are amusing themselves at backgammon and chess; the quick-blooded young men are fencing. Under a pine tree near an eglantine they have set a throne of pure gold, and there sits the King who rules sweet France. His beard is white and his hair is in full flower. His body is noble and his bearing is princely. If a man were to come looking for him, there would be no need to point him out. (8)[1]

This is not description for its own sake; its aim is specifically to place the narrative and make it immediate. The unforgettable lines that precede the arrival of the rear guard at the pass of Roncevaux provide another example:

The peaks are high and the valleys are dark, the gorges awesome under dun rocks. (66)

The same scene is described when Charles' army sets out to aid Roland:

The peaks are high and dark and huge, the valleys deep, and the torrents dash through them. They sound their trumpets at the head of the column and at the rear, and all together blare in answer to Roland's ivory horn. (138)

And again, as the death throes of the hero begin:

The mountains are high, and the trees are tall, and there are four great stones of marble there, shining. Count Roland faints on the green grass. (169)

These repetitions are clearly not accidental; they answer and echo one another from afar. The poet closely links the setting to the action as he sustains and intensifies the emotion. The re-

[1] The quotations in this chapter are taken from the translation of W. S. Merwin, in *Medieval Epics* (New York: Random House, Modern Library, 1963); reprinted by permission of Random House, Inc. Arabic numerals refer to strophe (*laisse*) numbers.

lation is schematic; but through repetition it becomes effective and, in its simplicity, takes on a vital significance. One long description would surely have been less effective.

The great military scenes of the *Chanson* provide a conclusion for these remarks. First, the description of the appearance of Marsile's troops:

> The pagans arm themselves in Saracen hauberks, most of them made of three thicknesses of chain mail. They lace their fine Saragossa helmets. The gird on their swords made of steel from Viana. They carry resplendent shields and Valencian lances with white and blue and crimson pennons. They leave behind their saddle mules and palfreys and mount their war horses and ride in closed ranks.
>
> The day was clear and the sun was fair. The light flashed from every piece of armor. A thousand trumpets are sounded, to add to the splendor. (79)

If the reader is indifferent to the accuracy of technical detail, he will perhaps appreciate the play of light or the correspondence between the bursts of color and the martial fanfare. The effect is all the more successful in that each aspect of the description represents a threat to the skill of the French. This passage can be compared to the strophe that describes Charlemagne's return to Roncevaux:

> The evening lengthens, the day draws out, and their armor shines against the sun, their hauberks and helmets flashing fire, and their shields also, which are elaborately painted with flowers, and their spears with the pennons worked in gold. (138)

The spectacle of Baligant's navy is even more magnificent:

They scud along with sails and oars, maintaining their course, and their mastheads and their tall prows gleam with carbuncles and lanterns which flash so brightly into the sky that at night they adorn the sea. And as the vessels approach the land of Spain, this brilliance floods the whole coast, so that it shines. (190)

This radiance expresses both the pride and the power of Islam. And here is the tumult of battle:

Huge are the hosts and fierce are their companies, and by now all of the battalions on both sides have met, and the pagans strike hard. Oh God, there are so many spear shafts splintered, shields smashed and mailed tunics burst apart! The ground is littered with them, and the green tender grass of the field. (244)

And if you had been there what a sight you would have seen of smashed shields, and what a din you would have heard of hauberks hacked apart and of shields grating against helmets. You would have seen knights falling, and men howling and dying on the ground, and you would have brought away a memory of great suffering! (253)

These awesome descriptions are complete — the chaotic impact of the troops, the voices rising over the fray, the weapons flashing in the air, the blood that stains the green grass. There is no unnecessary ornamentation. It is a restrained account in which each word has weight and meaning.

The author of the *Roland* knows how to describe a crowd. He can arrange battles and set down the elements of which they are composed. But he reveals a marked preference for single combat. The incidence of individual confrontations in his narrative is high; through repetition he probably intends to give the impression of furious animosities. More important, he wants to pay homage to personal worth and to show the courageous rivalry that impels the best to distinguish themselves from the crowd in battle. Although his use of the few available details is ingenious, they unfortunately reappear too often to remain interesting. Eventually the lances that shatter or pierce the flesh up to the pennon are boring; one tires of seeing the steel, gold, and gems of the helmets that shoot sparks under the impact of swords, of watching split skulls spill out their brains and entrails being exposed in waves of blood. A hierarchy of prowess ought to correspond to the hierarchy of the heroes. But, if the least of the Christian knights can be a superman, it becomes very difficult to illustrate the superiority of Roland, let alone Charlemagne. It is hardly surprising that some fantastic blows are amusing rather than impressive, but we should be cautious in speaking of clumsiness or naiveté. The medieval public was more aware than we of what a man with a sword could do, and our poet is much too interested in pleasing his audience to have gratuitously offended them. Because of his deep conviction of the nobility of his subject, he is committed to audacity and feels free to invent the most improbable exploits. We should believe only what he asks us to believe, however. If he offers an ecstatic description of muscular force, it is obvious that he admires it. But he admires it principally because it can reveal the unconquerable heroism of a soul, the militant fervor of faith, the victorious sanctity of a cause. Whoever embodies these moral forces and finds his very motive and end in God is, must be, capable of anything. This is the logic of the *Roland* poet: he no more feared contradiction than he doubted his talent.

Thus he does not hesitate to describe at length the duel between

Charlemagne and Baligant, though he is certainly running a risk. This duel must sum up the others without repeating or diminishing them. In particular, it must not detract from Roland's exploits. The passage itself will attest to the success of his attempt:

> The day passes, the evening comes, and Franks and pagans fight on with their swords. Those who have led these two hosts into battle are brave men. They have not forgotten their war-cries: the Emir shouts, "Precieuse!" and Charles raises his famous battle cry of "Mountjoy!" And by their clear ringing voices the two men recognize each other, and they meet in the middle of the field and ride to attack each other, and exchange heavy blows, each one's spear smashing into the other's ringed shield. And each shield is pierced above the broad boss, and the folds of both their hauberks are rent, but on neither side do the spears enter the flesh. Their cinches break and their saddles tip over and both kings fall to the ground, but they leap to their feet at once and bravely draw their swords. Now nothing can separate them, and the fight cannot end except with the death of one or the other.

> Charles of sweet France is gifted with great courage, and the Emir shows neither dread nor hesitation. They draw their swords, showing the naked blades, and they deal each other heavy blows on their shields, cutting through the leather coverings and the two outer layers of wood, so that the nails fall and the buckles are broken in pieces. Then, bare of shields, they hack at each other's coats of mail, and the sparks leap from their bright helmets. This combat cannot be brought to an end without one or the other confessing that he is wrong.

The Emir says: "Charles, consider the matter carefully and make up your mind to repent for what you have done to me. You have killed my son, if I am not mistaken, and you are wrongfully disputing with me the possession of my own country. If you will become my vassal [and swear fealty to me] you may come with me and serve me from here to the East."

Charles answers: "To my way of thinking that would be vile and base. It is not for me to render either peace or love to a pagan. Submit to the creed which God has revealed to us, become a Christian, and my love for you will never end as long as you put your faith in the omnipotent King and serve Him."

Baligant says: "You have begun a bad sermon!" Then they raise their swords and resume the fight.

The Emir is a strong and skillful fighter. He strikes Charlemagne upon his helmet of burnished steel and splits and smashes it above his head, bringing the sword down into the fine hair, sheering off a palm's breadth and more of flesh, and laying bare the bone. Charles staggers and almost falls, but it is not God's will that he should be killed or beaten. Saint Gabriel comes to his side, asking:

"Great King, what are you doing?"

When he hears the holy voice of the angel, Charles loses all fear of death, and his vigor and clearness of mind return. He strikes the Emir a blow with the sword of France, cleaves the helmet flashing with jewels, cuts open the head and spills the brains, and splits the whole face down through the white beard. It is a corpse, past all hope of recovery, which that stroke hurls to the ground. Charles calls "Mountjoy!" to rally his vassals, and at his shout Duke Naimes comes to him

bringing with him the Emperor's horse Tencendur, and the
King mounts.

The pagans flee. It is not the will of God that they should
remain. Now the French have achieved the triumph which
they had hoped for. (258–262)

Everything about this encounter recalls the previous battles. The
blows dealt by these two adversaries have already been exchanged
by others, in the same way and with the same effect. Others, like
them, have stopped for a moment to affirm their cause or to offer
a final appeal. Yet there is no doubt of the exceptional value of
this passage. The poet has allowed himself repetitions, but there
is no good reason to condemn in him what we admire in Homer.

The details or expressions that he has already used are skillfully
altered or reordered. His effort at composition, or synthesis if
you will, is rewarded and is all the more remarkable in that he
has not admitted unrealistic devices. What then explains the gigantic proportions of the scene? We should first recall its context, its place in the drama, and the opponents involved. Most
important is the element of supernatural intervention that is introduced to establish the scope; though subtle, it is the only occurrence of its kind in the entire poem. At the most critical moment
of the battle, it is to Charlemagne alone that God reveals himself.
He makes it clear that Charles is his champion, serving a cause
that is sacred among all others. To unite such grandeur and such
simplicity is hardly an easy task.

A further word now on characterization. Because of its unusual intensity, the portrait of Baligant immediately attracts attention. The poet has devoted a long strophe to him. Charlemagne's adversary is well worth such a tribute; and he is alone
among the pagans in deserving the eulogistic regret that concludes his portrait:

The Emir bestirs himself, not to be the last. He puts on his coat of mail with its gilt-varnished skirts, laces his helmet which is studded with jewels set in gold, and then girds his sword onto his left side. He has heard of Charles' sword, and his pride has found a name for his own: "Precieuse." The word has become his battle cry; he has commanded his knights to shout "Precieuse." He hangs from his neck his great broad shield with its golden boss and crystal border; it is swung on a thick strap of silk embroidered with circles. He grasps his spear named Maltet, with its shaft as thick as a club. Its iron head alone would make a full load for a pack mule. Then, while Marcules, from across the sea, holds his stirrup, Baligant mounts his war horse. He has a good broad stride in the saddle, this brave knight. He is narrow in the hips, but big-ribbed, and his chest is deep and beautifully molded, his shoulders are massive, his color is fair and his face proud. His curling hair is as white as a summer flower. His courage has been proved many times. God, what a baron, if only he were a Christian. (228)

Baligant may seem to be receiving preferential treatment, but in fact the poet has not neglected his favorite heroes. Since he is always near them, and assumes us also to be at their side, he does not feel the need to set down single, complete portraits. Their images become increasingly clear in our minds as we participate in the drama of which they are the protagonists. The concise sketches that bring them to life are surprisingly evocative and, in the course of the action, reveal more of their souls than their faces. The poet relates everything that he sees or hears to these souls: conversation, attitudes, acts of heroism or ignominy. Going beyond the poet as portrayer of character, let us examine the artistry that so successfully complements the psychology he uses.

A good place to start is with the portrait of Roland riding through the pass, proud, smiling, and uncorrupted, as befits the martyr that he will be in a few hours:

> Where the pass leads up out of Spain Roland has mounted Veillantif, his good swift horse. He has taken up his arms; his armor becomes him. Now with a flourish Roland the bold raises the point of his lance to heaven. Laced to the shaft is a white pennon whose fringes sweep down to his hands. He bears himself nobly; his countenance is candid and smiling. Behind him comes his companion, and the French, who regard him as their salvation. He turns and looks fiercely at the Saracens, and then humbly and sweetly at the French. (91)

There are many other shorter but no less expressive sketches. Here is Ganelon, first at the council scene, then before Marsile:

> And Count Ganelon is distraught. He throws off the great sable mantle from around his neck, and stands up in his silk shirt. His eyes are gray and his face is haughty; a noble carriage, a broad chest. He is so handsome that all the peers stare at him. (20)

> He is wearing a cloak of sable covered with Alexandrian silk. He flings it aside; Blancandrin catches it. But he keeps his sword, his right hand grasping the gold hilt.
> The pagans say: "Here indeed is a noble baron!" (35)

And here is Roland in the midst of battle:

> Count Roland rides over the field, with Durendal, that good carver and cleaver, in his hand, and he wreaks carnage among the Saracens. You would have seen him fling corpse upon corpse, and the clear blood cascading into pools. His hauberk

and both his arms, and the neck and shoulders of his horse, are covered with blood. (105)

The more important the character is, the more fragmented his portrait. This fragmentation is the result of an attempt to sustain a presence and to match the rhythms of life, and is even more true of Charlemagne's portrait than of Roland's. The emperor's attitudes are noted with care and consistency, and provide the most impressive and significant examples of the poet's style. Three magnificent lines serve to introduce the old sovereign:

His beard is white and his hair is in full flower. His body is noble and his bearing is princely. If a man were to come looking for him, there would be no need to point him out. (8)

While the barons argue, Charles is thinking, his head bowed; or, remote, he distractedly strokes his beard; suddenly he starts out of his reverie with a harsh look or an indisputable order which puts an end to the uproar and quarreling. In one scene he blesses his ambassador with the gesture of both king and priest; in another, he falls to the ground in prayer. At Roncevaux he wanders alone among the dead in search of Roland and then, leaning against a pine and supported by his barons, delivers his nephew's funeral eulogy. Confronted by Baligant, he regains his strength and rides proudly at the head of his troops, his white beard spread over his coat of mail. As Pauphilet has remarked, each of these attitudes reflects an instant in his interior life and reveals either his humanity or his grandeur. It is difficult to decide which of these many passages is the most moving or admirable.

The descriptions and portraits in the *Roland* are full of movement, color, and vitality, but they are valuable for other qualities as well. The idea of the exotic has already been introduced. It occurs, for example, in regions where the olive tree is found.

More important, it appears in the description of Baligant's squadrons. The poet piles up strange names and picturesque details with lavish enthusiasm. But the profusion and extravagance are neither gratuitous nor naive. Any picture of Islam and the East at the time of the First Crusade was bound to be approximate and tendentious. The author can hardly be blamed for sharing the ignorance and prejudices of his contemporaries. Quite the contrary, he should be praised for his artistic interpretation of the material provided by the oral and clerical traditions. In his descriptions he has included imaginary as well as actual characters and has given them names. Reality is not the only source of poetic inspiration; fantasy is also important, and giants and monsters are not out of place in the epic. The author of the *Roland* confronts his task and takes full advantage of the available possibilities. Since the drama of Roncevaux is far from ordinary, he must lead the reader beyond his usual perspective. From recollection, imagination, and a crusader's enthusiasm, he has constructed these extraordinary beings who are incarnations of the spirit of evil. His descriptions are bold and sure and sometimes achieve a verbal power that in itself justifies their creation, even though his persistence risks offending our taste. The following example shows the effect he can get from a bizarre detail or a sonorous name:

> The first is made up of warriors from Butenrot; the one which follows it is composed of vassals from Micenes, with big heads. Like hogs, they have bristles all along their spines. And the third battalion contains the vassals from Nubles and Blos, and the fourth those from Bruns and Esclarons, and the fifth those from Sobres and Sores, and the sixth the Armenians and the Moors, the seventh the Knights from Jericho, the eighth those from Nigres, the ninth those from

Gros, and the tenth is made up of vassals from the stronghold of Balide, whose people have always been a race of malefactors. (232)

Neither the marvelous nor the fantastic can unsettle such a vigorous and flexible talent. Although the *Roland* poet is working in a tradition that goes back to biblical and pagan antiquity, he is capable of great originality. Since the marvels that announce Roland's death are so well known, I shall quote instead Charlemagne's dream on the eve of the second battle of Roncevaux:

Charles looks up toward heaven and sees thunderbolts, hail, rushing winds, storms and awesome tempests, and fires and flames appear to him, falling suddenly upon his whole army. The lances of ash wood and of apple wood catch fire and burn, and the shields, even to the gold bosses on them. And the shafts of their sharp spears are splintered, and their hauberks and their steel helmets are broken; and he sees his knights in great distress. Then bears and leopards come to devour them, serpents and vipers, dragons and devils, and more than thirty thousand griffons, and all of them fling themselves on the French. (185)

We can expect no less from an intelligence and an imagination that we already know to be capable of so much. The question is only whether the poet exhibits a lack of moderation or control. The truth is that he uses the fantastic; he does not abuse it. The description of Baligant's troops is the only one of its kind in the poem. Dreams, miracles, and marvels are the exception, as they should be. We have noted the subtlety with which supernatural intervention is described. A few shortcomings, of which we are perhaps bad judges, count for little next to so many successes.

Edmond Faral has remarked that the *Roland* poet's concept of literary effect leads him to dwell on the most important and moving situations, instead of following events as they occur. The *Chanson* is less a narrative than a sequence of scenes. It is essentially dramatic, which no doubt explains its sustained excitement.

Let us go back to the first act of the poem. The two initial scenes that contrast the courts of Marsile and Charlemagne are clearly the work of a dramatist. The dialogue is central, the style direct. A few descriptive remarks appear here and there, but only where they are needed to establish the scene, describe the surroundings, and introduce the characters. First is Marsile's council: of a total of eighty lines, nine serve as introduction, five establish the setting, and the rest are speeches or replies. A short transitional strophe takes us to Chalemagne's camp. The famous eighth strophe, which was quoted earlier and is only a little longer, then names and places the characters. In the center, on his golden throne, is the emperor; near him are Roland, Oliver, Anseis, Geoffroy, Gerin, and Gerier. On rugs of white silk the oldest knights play backgammon and chess; to one side, the youngest fence. The light is directed toward the throne, which is sheltered by a pine, and is focused on its occupant. This description is dramatic and is thus a highly appropriate introduction to a debate — the debate that will lay the way for the catastrophe. The protagonists have only to come forward and speak. As in the theater, they reveal their characters and the causes of the action through their replies and tirades. Dramatic devices, such as stage directions for an action or attitude, accompany only the decisive speeches: Roland himself springs up to be the first to speak his mind and to utter a burst of scornful laughter; Ganelon throws off his sable cloak and lets fall the glove that is entrusted to him; Charlemagne lowers his head and strokes his white beard when he is anxious, roughly separates the peers, and solemnly blesses his messenger. The anonymous crowd of barons approves or comments as would an ancient chorus. Very well, one might say — and what is true of the first council of the French is true of the second, and also of Ganelon's mission to Marsile. But is not the *Chanson* primarily the story of a two-stage battle?

In fact, the style of the poem does not change radically when the action shifts to Roncevaux. The poet does not recount Charles' march across the mountains. Rather, he shows him in the sinister setting of the pass. He is explaining his anxiety to Duke Naimes, who has questioned him. Dialogue recurs during Marsile's preparations for battle, and it is hardly necessary to point out again the two quarrels between Roland and Oliver. The unforgettable battle is broken up into several stages, and most often each stage consists of a series of single engagements. We are not offered a continuous narrative, but a collection of little scenes that focus attention on specific areas of the battle-field or on a particular pair of adversaries. And in the *Roland* men speak almost as much as they fight; before the battle or even in the midst of the struggle, there is time for challenge, repri-mand, exhortation, monologue, and debate. Such a succession of animated, striking dramatic images inevitably recalls the tech-nique of modern cinema: the fragmented action and shifting per-spective are similar, as is the convergence of means and effects in an attempt to create a total illusion of life. Certainly this tech-nique was well suited to the mimed declamation of the jongleurs who were entrusted with the oral transmission of the chansons.

If dialogue is so important, it must be pointed and sparing in its effect. As the more famous scenes of the poem show, the speeches follow a deliberate pattern; each person says only what

he has to say, at the right time, and in terms which can best
reveal his character or explain his actions. The remark that sets
the drama in motion is extremely theatrical. Before Roland utters
the remark, "Let it be Ganelon, my stepfather," we are at the
most critical point in a heated discussion, a moment of extreme
tension. These elements combine to give an incalculable weight
to the words about to be spoken. Roland is either unaware or
uninterested, but the poet has weighed each of the words the
hero uses. Ganelon's hasty reply, "I am your stepfather, as everyone knows," foreshadows the parallel scene that results in Roland's designation: "Let it be Roland, my stepson." These inter-
dependent replies, set off by verbal parallels, explain and control
the action and make the *Roland* a true drama. There is no need
to add that in this drama the tirades and speeches are as remarkable as the best dialogue. A few lines suffice for Roland and
Ganelon to explain their reactions to Marsile's offers. More could
not be said with fewer words:

[Roland] says to the King: "If you believe Marsiliun you
will live to regret it. Here we have been for seven whole
years in Spain, and I have conquered Noples and Commibles
for you, and Valterne and the country of Pine, and Balasgued
and Tudele and Sezilie. And King Marsiliun has already betrayed us. He sent fifteen of his pagans, each carrying an
olive branch, and they all said these same words to you.
And you did as your Franks suggested — they must have
been lightheaded when they advised you. You sent two of
your counts to the pagan, one of them was Basan and the
other Basilie. He cut off their heads there in the mountains
below Haltilie. Carry on with this war as you began it.
Take the host which you have assembled and attack Sara-

gossa and lay siege to the city. Let the struggle continue for the rest of your life, if necessary, but avenge those whom this villain murdered."

. . . None of the Franks says a word, except Ganelon . . . "You will live to regret it if you lend your ear to some good-for-nothing, myself or another, who does not have your best interests at heart. When King Marsiliun sends to tell you that he is willing to clasp hands and become your vassal, when he offers to rule all of Spain through your gift and says that he will submit to our law, then whoever tells you that we should reject his offer, Sire, does not much care what kind of death we may die. It is not right that the promptings of arrogance should prevail. Let us ignore the fools and cling to the wise!" (14–15)

At the beginning of the battle, Oliver expresses his wisdom and reason with the same conciseness:

The pagans have a huge army, and our French appear to be very few. Therefore, Roland, my companion, sound a blast on your horn. Charles will hear it, and he will return with his host. (83)

Finally, here is one of Charlemagne's speeches, delivered at the beginning of the second battle:

Barons of France, you are good vassals and you have fought many battles in the field. You can see the pagans: they are evil and cowardly and their whole credo will not do them a farthing's worth of good. What difference does it make, my lords, if they come in great numbers? If any man does not wish to come with me let him go now! (239)

These words clearly flatter, comfort, and inspire the French. They make heroism an obligation.

The poet's feeling for his subject is intense, and he wants us to experience it with the same fervor. As we have just seen, he first achieves this total participation by dramatic means. But it would be a mistake to overlook his other qualities, for they are no less valuable. His narrative and descriptive passages are as effective as his dialogue. Equally moving is his subtle but powerful lyricism, often expressed through *laisses similaires*. This form, which also appears in other chansons, consists of using the same group of themes and motifs, with some variation, in two or more successive verses. Practicality is not the only reason for these repetitions. The chansons were recited before a public that was boisterous and easily distracted; if the texts could not sustain or revive attention, they had at least to counteract their shortcomings with clever and timely repetitions. But what might have been mere expedience has been turned to marvelous account by our author, as can be seen in the three verses that describe Roland's last moments. Here are the first two:

Now Roland feels death taking everything from him, descending from his head into his heart, and he runs under a pine tree and lies down with his face to the green grass. Underneath him he places his sword and ivory horn. He turns his head toward the pagans, so that Charles and all his knights may say: "The noble knight died a conqueror."

He makes his confession, carefully, over and over, and he offers his glove, as a token of his sins, to God.

Now Roland feels that the end of his life has come. He has lain down on a steep hill with his face toward Spain and with one hand he beats his breast:

"God, I acknowledge my guilt and I beg for Thy mercy

for all the sins, greater and lesser, which I have committed
from the hour of my birth until this day when I lie here
overcome by death!"
He has held out his right glove to God.
Angels descend out of heaven and come to him.

(174-175)

It could be said that these repetitions include slight changes
which, though they slow down the narrative, do not impede its
progress. Perhaps they detract from its clarity and strength. But
on the other hand they cast a powerful spell over the emotions,
for time is suspended. The crucial moment, which should be more
intensely experienced than the others, is prolonged, and this sus-
pension creates an unexpected depth. Attitudes, gestures, words,
and thoughts all take on a fuller and more personal meaning.
Our spirit joins that of the great hero and goes with him to
the threshold of eternity.

The poet would not have achieved the same effect if he had
disregarded the problem of form. But we must avoid anachronisms
in our appraisal of the *Roland*'s style, and should think both of
other chansons and of the austere grandeur of Romanesque
churches. We must not demand of our author's language or
meter a variety and flexibility that did not yet exist. The vocabulary of Old French was extensive but quite different from the
modern language. The syntactical logic was not as subtle; juxta-
position was more common than continuity. At such a distance
it is difficult to appreciate fully the quality and meaning of the
words or to understand all of their connotations. Of course we
are familiar with the structure of the epic decasyllabic line. The
strong caesura that breaks the line at the fourth syllable has not
lost its effect, nor has the assonance that marks its end; but the
frequency of the epic caesura, with its overcounted unstressed

syllable, is unusual. Moreover, though we know that these lines were sung or chanted, it would be difficult to say exactly what the rhythms or melodies were.

Still, to think that we were dealing with primitive poetry would be a mistake. The style of the *Chanson* reveals clerical influences; specifically it is not without similarities to contemporary epics in Latin. No single direct imitation of these highly artificial works — or of the *Aeneid* or the *Pharsalia*, for that matter — can be found in the *Roland*. Nevertheless, our author uses devices that are common in the technical jargon of the time: *oppositio* (it is true, it is not a lie), *amplificatio, interjecto ex persona poetae* (direct intervention of the poet), *addubitatio* (what should I do?), and *praemonitio* (preparation). He is familiar with apostrophe, hyperbole, the rhetorical question, alliteration, and understatement. He knew the Bible and has borrowed certain phrases from theological language. Such words as *meie culpe, paterne, Lazaron,* and *resurrexis* are taken from the Latin text of the Mass. But, having rejected one extreme, we should not go to the other: though the style of the *Roland* is not primitive, it is not erudite.

The *Roland* avoids labored affectation and unnecessary weight. Its style is marked by conciseness, precision, sparseness, and strength. This degree of austerity and steadiness presupposes a certain rigidity and monotony. The author was not familiar with such devices as the periodic sentence or enjambement, and prefers asyndeton to subordination; he tends to make an independent and self-sufficient unit of each line. This apparent fragmentation is offset by the fact that parallels, contrasts, and logical or intuitive implications link these units into considerably larger groups. Lines that are admirable in themselves are even better in context. The poet's vocabulary has the advantage of being simple and precise: he respects words. He does not waste them or weaken them by excessive or inexact use. He has no need for esoteric terms; the right word, with all its possible connotations, is enough for him. A good example is the famous line, "Roland is bold and Oliver is wise" (*Rollant est proz e Oliver est sage*). These ordinary epithets could hardly be applied with more force. When they appear, we are already familiar enough with the characters to know that the words describe them fully, without simplifying. As the action proceeds, we realize that this antithesis not only reveals the cause of the drama but also explains its evolution and determines the tragic results. And when the poet completes his description of the heroes by adding, "Both of them are renowned for their bravery" (*Ambedui unt merveillus vasselage*), he is not praising them in general terms. He evokes and embodies an ideal, creates a total epic atmosphere through these unique characters. The author of the *Roland* is clearly one of the first to have used the French language artistically. He has at his disposal an instrument that has not been dulled by the quest for literary effect, and he has had to learn how to handle the instrument himself. This advantage has not made his task any easier, but his success fully justifies any effort.

Since the vitality of the poet's style comes from the careful selection and location of words, he is able to avoid the use of imagery and simile. Both are very rare in the *Chanson*; at most he says that a horse is as swift as a swallow or a falcon, or that Charles' beard is flowing, whiter than an April flower or snow on ice. Only once is he more insistent: "As stags before the dogs, the pagans run before Roland." A writer who so carefully avoids description for its own sake must sacrifice unnecessary ornamentation to what he deems essential. Yet this same writer, so sober, so austere, and so careful in his use of words, is free in his use of repetitions and synonyms. It would be paradoxical to assume that this can be explained as carelessness. Certain epithets, descriptions, and formulas reappear throughout the *Roland*. Phrases like the following are common: "par honur e par ben," "a hunte e a viltet," "vieill e al canut," "curuçus e irez" — as are several tautologies: "Carles se dort, qu'il ne s'esveillet mie," "Morz est li quens, que plus ne se demuret." But we must remember that repetition is a very important aspect of the poet's technique, as in the *laisses similaires*. The recurrence of a characteristic adjective can show the permanence of those very moral or physical qualities that define an individual. As an example, let us look at Charlemagne's beard, at the old monarch's pensive attitudes when he is frightened or uncertain. The majesty of his face is immutable, his spiritual anguish always deeply moving: there is no need to search for new words. Synonyms and recurring expressions can stress the depth and intensity of an emotion. The poet does not use excess phrases or padding; he strives for strength and clarity of expression. But he knows that the complexity of emotions and ideas requires the association of a number of terms that complement or qualify one another. And he knows that certain words are charged with emotional overtones. By the rhythmic incantation of repetition, which modifies the meaning as it augments it, he both intensifies and prolongs these innuendos. Some of his lines are the most evocative and suggestive in the French language. It has been said that many chansons, in which the flaws of a formulary style abound, are the product of a kind of perpetual oral improvisation, but that observation has no application here.

This brief analysis will best be concluded by focusing attention once again on the text itself, for we find the most perfect expression of the poet's artistry in the third of the three strophes that describe Roland's death.

Li quens Rollant se jut desuz un pin;
Envers Espaigne en ad turnet sun vis.
De plusurs choses a remembrer li prist,
De tantes teres cum li bers conquist,
De dulce France, des humes de son lign,
De Carlemagne, sun seignor, kil nurrit;
Ne poet muer n'en plurt e ne suspirt
Mais lui meïsme ne volt mettre en ubli,
Cleimet sa culpe, si priet Deu mercit:
"Veire Paterne, ki unkes ne mentis,
Saint Lazaron de mort resurrexis
E Daniel des leons guaresis,
Guaris de mei l'anme de tuz perilz,
Por les pecchez que en ma vie fis!"
Sun destre guant a Deu en puroffrit.
Seint Gabriel de sa main l'ad pris.
Desur sun braz teneit le chef enclin;
Juntes ses mains est alet a sa fin.
Deux tramist sun angle Cherubin
E seint Michel del Peril;
Ensembl'od els sent Gabriel i vint.
L'anme del cunte portent en pareïs.

The scene described in these twenty-two lines comes at the conclusion of a skillful development: from now on, the meaning of
Roland's death and the reward it deserves are clear. Twice the
poet has shown the hero stretched out on a hill, in the shade of
a pine tree, his face turned toward Spain. By saying it a third
time at the beginning of the strophe, the poet shows that he is
not interested in merely describing a pose. He wants to remind
us that Roland dies justified and unconquered, fulfilling the vow
that he made before he fell in this strange land, far in front of

his men, facing the fleeing enemy. The magnificent epic and religious theme, illustrated by the hero's sacrifice and intensified by
rhythmic repetition, must resound at this supreme moment. But
the glorious, triumphant note is muted by melancholy. Roland's
nobility is the result of his pain. As he nears his death, the
martyr of Roncevaux thinks of all that binds him to earth and
life, and he glories in his conquests one last time. Without this
gentle regret, his sacrifice would be worthless. He also thinks of
"dulce France." Throughout the poem this expression is wrapped
in a cloud of nostalgia and proud tenderness: nowhere is it more
moving than when it is so simply repeated in this last farewell.
The slightest elaboration would destroy the meaning of the words
that follow: "des humes de son lign, / De Carlemagne, sun seignor,
kil nurrit." In their laconic eloquence they sum up all of Roland's
emotions, all the reasons for his sorrow. They are spoken slowly.
The dying man lingers over his memories and tries to prolong
each precious moment as his sadness slowly gives way to serene
resignation.

But melancholy leads to forgetfulness. Roland's life has involved not only precious and beautiful memories, but also faults
that must be pardoned. The man must give way to the Christian,
to repentance and faith. Roland realizes that he barely has enough
time in which to pray. His prayer is short but intensely poignant,
the essence of an old prayer for the dead. With as much solemnity as audacity, it translates the Latin formulas into the vernacular and yet, because there is less need for eloquence than for
sincerity and contrition, it remains remarkably simple. When the
prayer is over, Roland acts out his speech, repeating his act of
penance and homage: once more he holds out his glove and beats
his breast. His humility is that of a good vassal who has delivered
himself to his lord, and the fact that it takes this form is quite
appropriate. As a loyal vassal and a crusader faithful to the point

of martyrdom, there is no better way for Roland to express his reverence and faith. God, who wishes Roland's death to be more noble than all the others', accepts the symbolic offering of feudal Christianity that has served his cause so well. He sends his angels and saints to welcome the soul that is ready to depart from the earth. A mediocre writer would have found it difficult to resist the temptation of describing the celestial vision. Our poet confines himself to two concrete details, both of which men have the right and faculty to perceive. Roland's head falls back, and his hands are clasped together — that is all the poet presumes to describe. He barely suggests the presence of the ranks that descend from heaven. This unforgettable scene must not become a spectacle. It must be as perfectly sacred and spiritually pure as the lofty sentiment that inspires it. The actual words that describe it have become immaterial, speaking not to the eyes or to the imagination, but to the spirit.

The author of the *Roland* was a great poet, both vital and sensitive, who knew his craft. He meant each strophe to form a whole and was free to determine the length of his verses. His skill in introducing and concluding them is evident in the sustained unity of tone. With the *—i* assonance he emphasizes the melancholy but triumphant aspect of the strophe just discussed. Because of the two strong beats at the fourth and tenth syllable, the lines progress with a majesty that does not preclude the occasional use of a more flexible rhythm. Each line is composed of two unequal parts. The first part stands alone and, despite its brevity, expresses the essential meaning of the line. After a strong caesura, the second carries over the sounds of the initial modulation and, if there is room, amplifies or develops them. The assonance stresses the ending of an individual line, while its timbre links it to the other lines. We cannot know the extent to which singing would have emphasized the meaning of the lines. The repetition of a single melody for each line of every strophe would have proved a severe limitation to the initiative of the performer. Still, this monotonous melody may well have expressed other nuances or stylistic effects. Our ignorance compels us to reserve judgment, but it does not keep us from admiring the stark rhythms or from paying tribute to the artist who used them to affirm the perfection of his skill.

NINE · CONCLUSION

Perhaps a measure of clarification can best be achieved by summarizing the assertions and doubts that have been expressed in this study.

In the final analysis, it is possible to assert the pre-excellence of the Oxford *Roland* with more certainty than ever. Its superiority is due not only to the fact that the Bodleian manuscript is the oldest and best known, but also to the exceptional quality of the text it transmits. This fact seems obvious in some respects, but it is still difficult to explain. The unknown poet was not one to lay bare his intentions. Painstaking analysis and delicate discussion are necessary to appreciate the structure of the *Chanson*, but this effort never goes unrewarded. Behind each decision we wish to understand, we glimpse a logic that never permits itself a mistake, even when its methods are obscure. In the process of discovering this organizing will, capable of both astonishing intuition and subtle calculation, we encounter a spirit that is led by its ideal to the highest peaks of heroism and faith, and yet remains close and immediate. Though it is set in the mythic perspective of an eternal crusade, the drama of Roncevaux never stops being human: it is organized by an architect but conceived by a portrait artist. And though the characters of the *Roland* attain super-human dimensions and are enveloped in a supernatural aura, they are linked to this world by their emotions. Each shapes his own destiny and, in fulfilling his particular fate, becomes an example and a symbol. As a result, the message that the characters convey is both unique and accessible.

Clearly a work so solidly constructed and so rich in ideas and implications could fulfill its potential only through a perfect efficacy of expression. The secret of this effectiveness is to be found in the conscious processes of a simple yet highly organized craftsmanship. The *Roland* poet makes use of many methods, but he avoids meaningless rhetoric and is never guilty of artifice. With as much expedience as tact, he selects his means and employs them toward his ends. His principal merit lies in the fact that he lives the drama he has invented. The intense participation he offers and inspires explains the high degree of pathos that his narrative so often achieves, and is responsible for the fact that his style — sober, understated, sparse, classic in its austerity and precision — evokes profound echoes. Of course the language of the *Chanson* remains too distant for us to pretend to apprehend all of its implications. But although the value of a word or the meaning of a line might be uncertain, there is no doubt about the poet's constant and pervasive mastery. The wealth of the most perfect works of art can never be fully explored, and the *Chanson de Roland* is no exception to the rule.

However reassuring it might be, this statement in itself cannot be intellectually satisfying. Whether we like it or not, it is an indication of the persistent limitations on our knowledge. There is a good chance that the *Roland* was composed shortly after the First Crusade and that its author was named Turoldus. But who was this great poet, and where did he come from? He refers with particular fervor to the Franks of France, and his culture is as broad as his technique is expert. This is too little, however, to allow us to say that he came from Ile-de-France or that he was a clerk rather than a jongleur. There is still a more serious problem. If legends about Roland existed, we know nothing about their content or their form, whether oral or written. We assume that a *Chanson de Roland*, other than that of the Oxford manuscript, already existed around 1050. But although the discoveries of recent years confirm the existence of this poem, they give us only the most meager details about it. It could not have been devoid of merit, but it is impossible to say more. Though we admit that from the middle, or even the beginning, of the eleventh century one or several narratives celebrated Roland's tragic death, the fact remains that, between the event of 15 August 778 and this relatively late literature, a hiatus exists that we cannot yet breach. Whether we discuss *complaintes* or *cantilènes*, legends that are widespread or localized in sanctuaries, oral or written sources, latent states or individual and distinct initiatives, even mutations, the results do not change. The genesis of the themes and means of expression of which the author of the *Roland* was able to take such remarkable advantage remains a mystery. We are not in a position to judge his originality.

As a matter of fact, it does not diminish his merit to see him as part of a long tradition. What is significant is to determine the importance and worth of what he added himself. He may have profoundly modified or reconstructed a mediocre model, or perhaps he organized for the first time an amorphous body of material. On the other hand, he might have transformed what was already an admirable poem into a masterpiece, with his gifts as a writer and an artist. The pervasive spirit in the *Chanson* seems to be truly his own, but it might well have been enriched by contact with other sources, to which he must in some measure owe the intensity of his emotions, the magnitude of his inspiration, the effectiveness of his appeal. Some people will never be satisfied at not being able to resolve these essential problems, and their regrets would be more than legitimate if they were accompanied by modesty and prudence. But whoever sincerely admires the *Chanson de Roland* must accept the ignorance and uncertainty without bitterness or resentment, for this mystery can make the work more precious to us. If we respect its secrets and are still sensible of its beauty, we preserve that almost providential quality that makes it — to use Bédier's term — the most precious of relics.

In fact, the Oxford *Chanson de Roland* is a relic, because of the near-miraculous aspects of its creation and content, because of its unique development. It was famous from the first years of the twelfth century and was soon imitated and translated: all the extant French and foreign versions of the Roland narrative are descended from it. The revisions it inspired were not equal to it, but they supplanted it because its language soon seemed archaic and audiences had come to prefer rhyme to assonance. The content also suffered from this modernization. Episodes were protracted, new scenes introduced. From 1150 on, the rivalry and subsequent triumph of the romance brought about a rapid decline in the epic itself. Charlemagne and Roland were not forgotten, but they were drawn with different faces. Other heroes were preferred, after the contemporary fashion, who were no less noble but were more *courtois*. Above all, the secret of the austere and vigorous art that created them and made them live was lost. They were then abandoned to the Spanish and Italian poets until that day in 1837 when Francisque-Michel published the Oxford manuscript. The resurrection was only complete with Bédier. We now share, with the contemporaries of the First Crusade, the privilege of knowing this admirable manuscript in almost perfect form. Reverence becomes an obligation. We must give the poet what he expects and ask for what he is prepared to give. If he finally makes a game of excessively scholarly concerns, he always responds to heights of inspiration that match his own. This is not to condemn the patient research of the last hundred years, but to draw a lesson from its failures as well as its successes. The failures are perhaps only temporary and are offset by the successes which, if they do not provide all the answers, at least allow us to understand and admire the essence of the poem.

BIBLIOGRAPHICAL NOTE
AND WORKS CITED

THE TEXT

The Oxford manuscript has been made easily accessible by a fine publication of the Société des Anciens Textes Français: *La Chanson de Roland*, a photographic reproduction of the Digby 23 manuscript from the Bodleian Library, edited by Count Alexandre de Laborde, with a historical and paleographical study by Charles Samaran (Paris, 1932).

The various versions of the poem, foreign as well as French, have been carefully reproduced by Raoul Mortier in *Les Textes de la Chanson de Roland,* 10 vols. (Paris: La Geste Francor, 1940–1949).

Among the critical editions, we should mention, in addition to that of Francisque Michel (1837), the following:

Theodor Muller, *La Chanson de Roland* (Göttingen: Dieterich, 1851–78).

Léon Gautier, *La Chanson de Roland* (Tours: A. Mame, 1872); frequently reprinted.

Edmund Stengel, *Das altfranzösische Rolandslied* (Leipzig: T. Weicher, 1900).

Gustav Groeber, *La Chanson de Roland* (Strasbourg: Heitz, 1908).

T. A. Jenkins, *La Chanson de Roland* (Boston: D. C. Heath, 1924).

Alfons Hilka, *Das altfranzösische Rolandslied* (Halle: M. Niemeyer, 1926); reviewed by Rholfs in 1948.

Giulio Bertoni, *La Chanson de Roland* (Florence: L. S. Olschki, 1936).

Joseph Bédier, *La Chanson de Roland, publiée d'après le manuscrit d'Oxford et traduite* (Paris: Piazza, 1922; 165th edition, 1947); the most important edition. Also *La Chanson de Roland commentée* (Paris: Piazza, 1927).

One of the most recent critical editions is that of Aurelio Roncaglia, in *Testi e manuali* (Modena: Società tipografica modenese, 1947).

It would not be inappropriate at this time to mention the principles that have guided the various editors in their work. In Chapter One I noted that, despite the incontestable superiority of the Oxford manuscript, it is far from perfect. The question then is to determine to what extent its text can be emended on the basis of the other versions. It was long assumed that the Oxford manuscript and the beginning of the V^4 manuscript, both of which are assonant, could have arisen from the same original. The rhymed versions would then consist of two families, growing out of another that was descended from the archetype. If we also include the foreign versions, we end up with a system that is clearly explained through the diagram adopted by Stengel and Foerster (see facing page). Within the framework of such a hypothesis, it would be legitimate to reject all O readings that are contradicted both by V^4 and any one of the other versions. Similarly, all readings common to O and V^4 that do not agree with at least two other parallel readings should be considered as apocryphal. In fact, in a sequence of evidence that goes back by various routes to the same original, all that is needed to eliminate one reading is for two to agree in their contradiction of it.

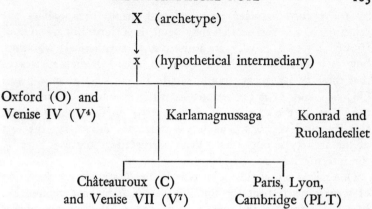

Since Bédier's time, after the 1930s, the situation has been assessed in a completely different way, as the following diagram shows:

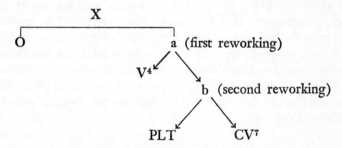

Here, instead of a system with five branches, we are presented with only two families, one of which consists solely of the unique Oxford manuscript. In this case, no reading from any of the derivatives of intermediary *a*, whether direct or indirect, and indeed no reading that is shared by several of these derivatives, is of any greater value than the unique and divergent reading of *O*. In other words, whenever *O* disagrees with one or several rival versions, its testimony alone carries as much weight as that of all the other versions combined. It is thus impossible to justify by the accord between two different manuscript families the rejection of any variant that may occur in a third. But when confronted by two equally authoritative, if antithetical, witnesses, how is it possible to choose between them? Bédier assures us that these two witnesses ought not to be put on the same plane. On one hand, O is not wrong as often as one might wish; on the other, in the case of an obvious error in O, nothing proves that the rival versions provide the correct solution, for the text of the archetype might have been corrected or restored here by the intermediary a.

One might say at this point that Bédier has made an obligation of scrupulous respect for the text of the *précellent* manuscript. In a few instances, the most recent editors have considered this respect to be excessive. They have based their corrections of O either on other versions or on conjecture. They think that O can and must be emended when its text raises legitimate suspicions, and these suspicions are confirmed by an examination of the other manuscripts. If V^4, in particular, offers a variant that fits perfectly into the context from the point of view of both form and content, they have no scruple about accepting it. This is why the latest critical editions do not strictly follow Bédier's. It is also why the differences between them are minor, since the choices they have had to make are more or less a matter of personal opinion.

TRANSLATIONS

Modern translations are numerous and exist in all languages. Aside from those that Léon Gautier and Joseph Bédier have included in their editions, the versions in modern French by Henri Chamard (1919) and Maurice Tessier (1944) are noteworthy. The most readable version in English is W. S. Merwin's, in *Medieval Epics* (New York: Modern Library, 1963).

SECONDARY WORKS

A number of bibliographical efforts have been devoted to the *Chanson de Roland*, and a list of them is to be found in the *Manuel bibliographique de la littérature française du moyen âge* by Robert Bossuat (Paris: Librairie d'Argences, 1951, 1955, 1961). This manual also contains an excellent listing of the principal character studies, general and particular, published to date. The *Bulletins bibliographiques*, published since 1958 by the Société Rencesvals (for the study of romance epics), should also be consulted.

If we limit ourselves, in listing the old publications, to those that are still of considerable interest and, in listing the new, to those that actually do say something new, we end up with the following list, in chronological order:

Gaston Paris, *Histoire poétique de Charlemagne* (Paris: E. Bouillon 1865, 1905). The great work that has served as a point of departure for all subsequent research and that propounded the theory of the *cantilènes*.

Léon Gautier, *Les Epopées françaises*, 3 vols. (Paris: V. Palmé, 1865–1868), and in 4 vols. (Paris, 1878–1894). Allows the *Roland* to be placed in the midst of the epic activity in the Middle Ages.

Pio Rajna, *Le Origini dell'epopea francese* (Florence, 1884).

Joseph Bédier, *Les Légendes épiques*, 4 vols. (Paris: Champion, 1908–1913 and 1914–1921). The third volume is devoted to Charlemagne and Roland; Bédier has skilfully explained his theory of the pilgrim routes and has also provided an admirable literary commentary on the first part of the *Chanson*.

Prosper Boissonnade, *Du nouveau sur la Chanson de Roland* (Paris: Champion, 1923). While objecting to Bédier, he attempts to identify places and characters in the poem by a geographical and historical study of the eleventh- and twelfth-century crusades in Spain; the results are often questionable.

Ferdinand Lot, "Etudes sur les légendes épiques françaises, V, *La Chanson de Roland*," in *Romania*, 1928, pp. 357–380. It is here that the author criticizes Bédier's thesis, taking as his point of departure the fact that there is no mention of the pilgrimage of Saint-Jacques in the Oxford version; whence his conviction that it is necessary to go back before the extant texts and assume the persistence of a memory or a tradition during the centuries.

Robert Fawtier, *La Chanson de Roland, étude historique* (Paris: Boccard, 1933). He stresses the importance of the event at Roncevaux itself and also tries to show the continuity of the recollection of the event; then he returns to the hypothesis of popular ballads composed on the day after the battle.

Albert Pauphilet, "*Sur La Chanson de Roland*," in *Romania*, 1933, pp. 161–198. Insists even more than Bédier on the determining role of the poet.

Edmond Faral, *La Chanson de Roland, étude et analyse* (Paris: Melottée, 1933). An excellent summary, which is interested in the problem of origins in order to defend Bédier's theories, but also views the poem as a work of art.

Giuseppe Chiri, *L'Epica latina medioevale e la Chanson de Roland* (Geneva: Emiliano degli Orfini, 1933). Attempts to show the dependence of the *Roland* on the medieval Latin epic.

Charles A. Knudson, "Etudes sur la composition de *La Chanson de Roland*," in *Romania*, 1937, pp. 48–92. The importance of the poet.

Raoul Mortier, *La Chanson de Roland, essai d'interprétation du problème des origines, quelques suggestions nouvelles* (Paris: Union latine d'éditions, 1939). Favors a Burgundian origin.

Maurice Wilmotte, *L'Epopée française, origine et élaboration* (Paris, 1939). An often excessive plea in favor of Latin origins. He believes in the continuity of classical traditions, through the intermediary of hagiographic narratives and scholarly epics, in the Middle Ages.

Henri Grégoire, in various works that are listed in the *Mélanges Hoepffner* (Strasbourg and Paris, 1949), has tried since 1939 to link the *Chanson* to the Norman expeditions in Epirus in the second half of the eleventh century.

Adrien Blanchet, "Les Monnaies dans *La Chanson de Roland*," in *Comptes rendus des séances de l'Ac. des Inscriptions*, 1942, pp. 36–48. Would fix the date of the poem between 1078 and 1090.

Emile Mireaux, *La Chanson de Roland et l'histoire de France* (Paris: Michel, 1943). A questionable argument that tries to extend the composition of the *Roland* over the period of a century and a half, from 1000 to 1150.

C. Guerrieri Crocetti, *La Chanson de Roland, problemi e discussioni* (Genoa: Di Stefano, 1946).

Albert Pauphilet, "La Date du *Roland*," in *Etudes romanes dédiées à Mario Roques* (Paris: Droz, 1946), pp. 7–14. Proposes the existence before 1064 of a poem similar to the one we know.

Charles A. Knudson, "The Problem of the *Chanson de Roland*," in *Romance Philology*, 1950.

Albert Pauphilet, *Le Legs du moyen âge* (Melun: Librairie d'Argences, 1950). Contains a fine chapter devoted to a literary analysis of the *Chanson*.

Italo Siciliano, *Les Origines des chansons de geste* (Paris: Picard, 1951). A very lively summary of the debate about origins.

Jules Horrent, *La Chanson de Roland dans les littératures française et espagnole au moyen âge* (Paris: Les Belles-Lettres, 1951).

Maurice Delbouille, *Sur la genèse de la Chanson de Roland* (Brussels: Palais des académies, 1954).

Martin de Riquer, *Les Chansons de geste françaises* (Paris: Nizet, 1957).

La Technique littéraire des chansons de geste (Paris: Les Belles-Lettres, 1959). Records of the International Colloquium held in September 1957 at Liège. Maurice Delbouille's study, "Les Chansons de geste et le livre," is particularly noteworthy.

René Louis, *L'Epopée française est carolingienne* (Saragossa: Publications of the Faculties of Philosophy and Letters, ser. II, no. 18, 1956).

Ramón Menéndez Pidal, *La Chanson de Roland y el neotradicionalismo* (1960); rev. ed. in French, *La Chanson de Roland et la tradition épique des Francs* (Paris: Picard, 1960). A monumental work in which the traditionalist theory finds its most complete and persuasive expression. For the reviews of this book or replies to it, see *Cahiers de civilisation médiévale*, 1961, pp. 269–291 (André Burger), and 1962, pp. 323–333 (Pierre Le Gentil); *Romania*, 1963, pp. 88–133 (Félix Lecoy).

André de Mandach, *La Geste de Charlemagne et de Roland*, 2 vols. (Geneva: Droz, 1961). The second volume deals with the *Pseudo-Turpin*.

The preceding works, particularly the last ones, can provide the necessary references and explanations for particular problems. The following works are also of interest:

On the *précellence* of *O*: André Burger, "Le Rire de Roland et la question rolandienne," *Cahiers de civilisation médiévale*, 1960, pp. 1–12, and 1961, pp. 269–291; Cesare Segre, "Tradizione fluttuante della *Chanson de Roland*," *Studi medievali*, 3rd ser., 1960, pp. 72–92.

On the Roland-Olivier couple: Rita Lejeune, "La Naissance du couple littéraire Roland et Olivier," *Mélanges Grégoire* (Brussels, 1950), II, 371–401; Paul Aebischer, *Revue belge de Philologie et d'Histoire*, 1953, pp. 657–675 and 1962, pp. 718–749 ("*La Chanson de Roland* dans le 'desert' littéraire du XIe siècle").

On Roland's sword, Durendal: Rita Lejeune, in *Mélanges M. Roques*, I, 149–167 (1951); E. B. Place, in *Modern Language Notes*, 1952, pp. 154ff.

On the monuments at Roncevaux and the pilgrimage of Saint-Jacques: Elie Lambert, in *Romania*, 1935, pp. 17–54, and 1946–47, pp. 363–387, and in *Bulletin hispanique*, 1935, pp. 417–436; Pierre David, in *Bulletin études portugaises*, 1945–1949.

On the musical aspects: Jacques Chailly, *L'Ecole musicale de Saint-Martial de Limoges jusqu'à la fin du XIᵉ siècle* (Paris, 1955).

On style and technique: The point of departure for recent research has been the provocative work of Jean Rychwer, *La Chanson de Geste. Essai sur l'art épique des jongleurs*, (Geneva-Lille: Droz-Giard, 1955).

Also noteworthy are *La Technique littéraire des chansons de geste*, cited above, and C. A. Robson, "Aux origines de la poésie romane, art narratif et mnémotechnie," *Moyen Age*, 1961, pp. 41–84.

The literary interpretation has only been discussed in relation to Roland's rashness: Alfred Foulet, "Is Roland Guilty of Démesure?" *Romance Philology*, 1957, pp. 145–148; Robert Guiette, in *Moyen Age*, 1963, pp. 845–855; J. H. White, "*La Chanson de Roland:* Secular or Religious Inspiration?" *Romania*, 1964, pp. 398–408; Eugène Vinaver, "La Mort de Roland, à la recherche d'une poétique médiévale," *Cahiers de civilisation médiévale*, 1964, pp. 133–143.

Finally, a fine work that discusses the iconography of the *Roland*: Rita Lejeune and Jacques Stiennon, *La Légende de Roland dans l'art du moyen age*, 2 vols. (Brussels: Arcade, 1966).

INDEX

Abd-al-Rahman, 14, 15
Abisme, 48
Aebischer, Paul, 34, 35, 41, 43, 72
Aeneid, 149
Agolant the African, 38
Aix, 22, 38
al-Arabi, Suleiman ben, 14, 15
Almoravides, 23
Alonso, Dámaso, 35, 36
Alphonse le Batailleur, 19
Alphonse VI of Spain, 23
Annales Royales, 11
Anseis, 130, 143
Anselm, 12, 13, 72
Antioch, battle of, 18
Ariosto, Ludovico, 1
Ascalon, battle of, 17
Astronome of Limoges, the, 12–13
Atilla, 30
Aucassin et Nicolette, 61
Aude, Roland's fiancée, 4, 7, 32, 100, 111

Baligant (Baligandus), emir: in *Pseudo-Turpin*, 38, 40; episode discussed, 42, 49–51, 93–98, 100, 128; and Charlemagne, 122, 128, 134–137; his forces described, 132–133, 141–142; characterized, 137–138; mentioned, 4, 11, 17, 20, 21, 40, 120, 140
Basan, 45, 79, 81, 83, 89
Baselius, 20
Basile, 45, 79, 81, 83, 89
Baudouin, 38, 40
Béchada, Grégoire, *Canso d'Antiocha*, 16
Bédier, Joseph: on "précellence" of Oxford *Roland*, 8, 47; on date of *Roland*, 17–18; on authorship of *Roland*, 24–25; on possible sources of *Roland*, 31; on reference to *Geste Francor* in *Roland*, 42–43; on evidence of oliphant and tombs, 43; on development of *chansons de geste*, 57–58, 60–62, 63, 64, 69–70; on Ganelon, 83, 84; on Roland at Roncevaux, 91; on Turoldus' skill, 126; quoted, 76; cited, 3, 24, 39, 66, 71, 77, 83, 87; mentioned, 40, 65, 74, 159
Béroul, Norman poet, 74
Bertolai, jongleur, 65
Bertrand, 36, 37
Béziers document, 33
Bibliothèque Nationale, 4, 5, 13, 28
Blancandrin: and Ganelon, 45, 46, 83, 85; role in *Roland*, 77, 78–79; mentioned, 40, 42, 51, 128, 139
Blaye, 7, 38, 39, 43, 51, 59
Bodleian Library, 3
Boiardo, Matteo, 1
Boissonnade, Prosper, 19, 20, 26, 59
Bordeaux, 51, 59
Bourdillon, Jean-Louis 4
Bramidoine, Queen, 94, 98
Brioude document, 33
Burger, André, 41, 43, 51, 61
Butentrot, Valley of, 17, 20

Cadiz, 38, 39
Campeu Charlyamen, 6
Canso d'Antiocha, 16
Cantar de mio Cid, 1
Cantares de gesta, 67
Cantilène de Saint Faron, 65
Cantilènes, 55, 56, 57, 64–65
Capella Caroli Magni, 31
Cappadocia, 17, 20
Carmen de prodicione Guenonis, 6–7, 41, 42, 46
Chailley, Jacques, 61
Chanson de Roland, La: first edition, 1–3; versions, 2–9; plot summarized, 10–11; based on historical event, 11–15; date of Oxford ms, 16–24; author, 24–26, 158–160; possible sources, 27–53, 158–160; Latin sources, 60; and *chansons de geste*, 71–75; structure, 100–102,